TRUE OR FALSE
Mind-Blowing Quiz

with

500+ FASCINATING FACTS
FOR SMART KIDS

to Explore Animals, the Human Body, Space, Our Planet, Science & the World's Best Kept Secrets!

MICHELLE BURTON

2024

WHAT'S INSIDE:

CHAPTER 7: INCREDIBLE INVENTIONS 146

CHAPTER 8: WORLD RECORDS AND UNBELIEVABLE ACHIEVEMENTS 163

ABOUT THE AUTHOR

 **Michelle Burton** has a special gift for turning everyday wonders into fascinating stories that spark the imagination and curiosity of young readers. As the happy mother of two curious kids, Michelle draws inspiration from her own children's questions, always striving to answer their "whys" and "hows" in the most captivating ways possible.

From a young age, Michelle was enchanted by the power of books. She would spend hours lost in stories, exploring distant lands, and learning about incredible facts. This early passion for reading led her to become an elementary school teacher, where she found joy in sharing the magic of learning with her students. Watching their eyes light up with curiosity and excitement inspired her to start writing her books.

Her goal is to turn every child who reads her books into a curious explorer of the world around him. Michelle believes that learning doesn't stop in the classroom - it's a lifelong journey that can happen anywhere and anytime.

In this book Michelle Burton invites young readers to embark on a journey of discovery. She hopes this book will not only provide answers to some of the most intriguing questions but also inspire children to ask their own and seek out the incredible knowledge that the world has to offer.

ACKNOWLEDGMENTS

Creating "True or False Mind-Blowing Quiz" has been an incredible journey, and it would not have been possible without the support and contributions of many wonderful people.

First and foremost, I want to thank my curious children, Michael and Marie, whose endless questions and thirst for knowledge inspired this book. Heartfelt thanks to my husband Andreas for his unwavering encouragement and patience during the countless hours spent researching and writing. Your love and support have been invaluable.

I am deeply grateful to my educators and librarians who have dedicated their lives to fostering a love of reading and learning in children. Your feedback and insights have helped shape this book into a resource that can inspire and educate young minds.

Finally, to the young readers and their families: thank you for choosing this book. I hope, that "Fascinating True or False Facts for Smart Kids" sparks your curiosity, ignites your imagination, and encourages a lifelong love of learning.

With gratitude,

Michelle Burton

CHAPTER 1: INTRODUCTION TO THE WORLD OF FASCINATING FACTS

Welcome to the "True or False Mind-Blowing Quiz with 300+ Fascinating Facts for Smart Kids"! Get ready to embark on an exciting journey through a world filled with curious questions and surprising answers.

This captivating book contains approximately 500 intriguing facts. Each fact is presented as a true or false statement that will challenge what you think you know about our amazing world. Underneath each fact, you'll find a detailed description and the correct answer, providing a deeper understanding and context to enhance the learning experience. Perfect for curious kids aged 7 to 13, this book promises hours of fun while challenging and expanding their knowledge about the world around them.

For Parents

Dear Parents,

Thank you for choosing " True or False Mind-Blowing Quiz " as part of your child's learning and entertainment journey. This book is created to captivate young minds with a blend of fun and education, making it an ideal resource for various occasions such as holidays, road trips, and daily learning adventures.

Here are a few tips to help you make the most of this book with your child:

- ✓ **Engage in Shared Learning**: Spend quality time exploring true or false facts with your child. Turn each fact into a fun quiz or game. Ask your child what they think before revealing the answer, and encourage them to explain their reasoning. This promotes analytical thinking and verbal skills.

- ✓ **Connect to Real Life**: Relate the facts to real-life experiences. Consider visiting a zoo or a nature reserve if you read about a particular animal. If the topic is about space, try stargazing together on a clear night.

- ✓ **Travel Companion**: Use this book as an engaging travel companion. The format is perfect for car rides, plane trips, or any journey, providing an entertaining and educational way to pass the time.

- ✓ **Fun Challenges**: Make learning interactive by creating fun challenges. For instance, quiz each other or set up a family true or false trivia game. This not only reinforces learning but also makes it an enjoyable family activity.

- ✓ **Encourage Curiosity**: Encourage your child to ask questions about the facts they find most interesting. Look up additional information together, fostering a habit of inquiry and a love for lifelong learning.

We hope this book becomes a cherished part of your child's educational journey, sparking their imagination and fueling their passion for knowledge.

Our Exclusive Bonus for You

As a special thank you for your purchase, we're thrilled to offer you a FREE digital "True or False Quiz about Science and Experiments".

Enjoy **over 20 exciting physics and chemistry experiments** using everyday household items!

How to Get Your Gift:

> ➢ Leave a review on this book on **http://www.amazon.com** sharing your thoughts and experiences about the book:

Positive ratings, reviews, and suggestions from interested people like you help others to feel confident about choosing this book and help us provide great books.

> ➢ Receive your exclusive "True or False Quiz with Interesting Home Science Experiments" **absolutely FREE.**

Use a link below or a QR Code:

https://BookHip.com/NJWFVBD

THANK YOU IN ADVANCE FOR YOUR REVIEW!

CHAPTER 2: AMAZING ANIMALS

2.1 Majestic Mammals

Explore the world of mammals, from the mighty elephants of the African savannah to the agile dolphins in the oceans. Learn about the unique characteristics that make mammals special, such as their warm-blooded bodies, fur, or hair, and how they nurse their young.

Fact: *Elephants are the only mammals that can't jump.*

Elephants are indeed the only mammals that cannot jump. Their body structure and immense weight prevent them from lifting all four feet off the ground simultaneously. **True**

Fact: *Bats are blind.*

Bats are not blind. While many species have poor eyesight, they rely heavily on echolocation to navigate and hunt in the dark. **False**

Fact: *All mammals give birth to live young.*

Most mammals give birth to live young, but there are exceptions. Monotremes, such as the platypus and echidna, lay eggs instead. **False**

Fact: *Dolphins communicate using a complex language of clicks and whistles.*

Dolphins use a sophisticated system of clicks, whistles, and body language to communicate with each other, demonstrating high levels of intelligence and social interaction. **True**

Fact: *The blue whale is the largest animal to have ever lived.*

The blue whale holds the record for being the largest animal ever known to have existed, reaching lengths of up to 100 feet and weights of over 200 tons. **True**

Fact: *Koalas drink water regularly from rivers and lakes.*

Koalas rarely drink water; they get most of their hydration from eucalyptus leaves. The name "koala" even comes from an Aboriginal word meaning "no water". **False**

Fact: *Kangaroos can only hop forward, not backward.*

Kangaroos are built for forward motion with their powerful hind legs and large feet, making it difficult for them to move backward. **True**

Fact: *Polar bears have white fur to blend in with their snowy environment.*

Polar bears actually have black skin and transparent fur. The fur appears white because it reflects visible light, helping them blend into their icy surroundings. **False**

Fact: *Dolphins can recognize themselves in a mirror.*

Dolphins are among the few animals that can recognize themselves in a mirror. This self-awareness is a sign of high intelligence, similar to humans, great apes, and elephants. **True**

Fact: *Cows have four stomachs to help them digest their food.*

Cows have one stomach with four compartments: the rumen, reticulum, omasum, and abomasum. This complex system helps them efficiently digest tough plant material. **False**

Fact: *Platypuses use their bills to detect electric fields produced by their prey.*

Platypuses have electroreceptors in their bills that allow them to detect the electric fields generated by the movements of their prey in the water, making them excellent hunters even with their eyes closed. **True**

Fact: *The giant panda's diet consists almost entirely of bamboo.*

Giant pandas primarily eat bamboo, making up over 99% of their diet. They can consume up to 40 pounds of bamboo daily to meet their nutritional needs. **True**

Fact: *Whales are fish.*

Whales are not fish; they are mammals. Unlike fish, whales breathe air through their lungs, give birth to live young and nurse their babies with milk. **False**

Fact: *Male lions do most of the hunting for their pride.*

Female lions do most of the hunting for the pride. They work together to stalk and capture prey, while male lions primarily protect the pride and its territory. **False**

Fact: *Platypuses lay eggs.*

Platypuses are one of the few mammals that lay eggs. Along with echidnas, they belong to a group called monotremes, which are egg-laying mammals. **True**

Fact: *Polar bears have white fur to blend in with their snowy environment.*

Polar bears**Fehler! Textmarke nicht definiert.** actually have black skin and transparent fur. The fur appears white because it reflects visible light, helping them blend into their icy surroundings. **False**

Fact: Giraffes sleep standing up.

Giraffes often sleep standing up to escape from predators if needed quickly. They can also sleep lying down but usually only do so when they feel safe. **True**

Fact: Humans are the only mammals capable of sweating to cool down.

While humans are unique in their ability to sweat profusely to regulate body temperature, some other mammals, like horses, also sweat to help cool down. However, most mammals use other methods such as panting. **False**

Fact: Sloths can take up to a month to digest their food.

Sloths have an extremely slow metabolism, and it can take up to a month for them to digest their food. This slow digestion is partly due to their low-energy diet of leaves. **True**

Fact: *Narwhals use their tusks for fighting.*

Narwhals primarily use their tusks, which are elongated teeth, for sensing their environment. The tusks have millions of nerve endings that help them detect changes in the water. **False**

Fact: *Otters hold hands while sleeping to keep from drifting apart.*

Sea otters often hold hands, or form "rafts," while sleeping to prevent drifting away from each other in the water. This behavior helps keep them safe and together. Sometimes, otters will also wrap themselves in kelp or seaweed. This natural anchor helps keep them in place and adds an extra layer of security against drifting away. **True**

2.2 Birds of a Feather

Discover the incredible diversity of birds, from the colorful parrots of the rainforests to the swift peregrine falcons. Understand how their unique adaptations, like hollow bones and specialized feathers, allow them to soar through the skies and thrive in various environments.

Fact: *All birds can fly.*

Not all birds can fly. Penguins, ostriches, and emus are examples of flightless birds. They have adapted to their environments in other ways, such as swimming or running. **False**

Fact: *Hummingbirds can fly backward.*

Hummingbirds are the only birds that can fly backward. Their unique wing structure allows them to hover, fly sideways, and even upside down. **True**

Fact: *Owls can rotate their heads almost completely around.*

Owls can rotate their heads up to 270 degrees. This extraordinary flexibility is due to special adaptations in their bones and blood vessels. **True**

Fact: *All birds have feathers.*

All birds have feathers, which are unique to them. Feathers provide insulation, aid in flight, and often play a role in mating displays. **True**

Fact: *The kiwi bird lays the smallest egg in relation to its body size.*

The kiwi bird lays one of the largest eggs in relation to its body size. Despite being about the size of a chicken, a kiwi's egg is almost as large as an ostrich egg. **False**

Fact: *Parrots can mimic human speech.*

Many parrots can mimic human speech and other sounds. They have a special vocal organ called the syrinx, which allows them to produce a wide range of sounds. **True**

Fact: *Woodpeckers peck at wood to find food and communicate.*

Woodpeckers peck at wood to find insects to eat, create nesting sites, and communicate with other woodpeckers through sound. **True**

Fact: *The albatross has the largest wingspan of any living bird.*

The wandering albatross holds the record for the largest wingspan of any living bird, reaching up to 12 feet. This helps them glide long distances over the ocean. **True**

Fact: *Birds have teeth.*

Birds do not have teeth. Instead, they have beaks and specialized digestive systems to help them break down food. **False**

Fact: *Flamingos are born pink.*

Flamingos are born with gray or white feathers. They turn pink due to the pigments in the algae and crustaceans they eat. **False**

Fact: *Pigeons can find their way home from long distances.*

Pigeons have an exceptional homing ability, allowing them to find their way back to their nests from long distances. They use the Earth's magnetic field and visual landmarks for navigation. **True**

Fact: *Penguins can fly underwater.*

Penguins are excellent swimmers and are often described as "flying underwater." Their flipper-like wings and streamlined bodies make them agile and fast swimmers. **True**

Fact: *The ostrich is the fastest-running bird.*

The ostrich is the fastest-running bird, capable of reaching speeds up to 45 miles per hour. Their long legs and strong muscles make them excellent runners. **True**

Fact: *Crows are not very intelligent.*

Crows are extremely intelligent birds. They can use tools, solve puzzles, and have excellent memory. Some studies suggest their cognitive abilities are on par with those of great apes. **False**

Fact: *Swans mate for life.*

Swans are known for forming long-term monogamous pairs. Many swan species mate for life, often returning to the same nesting site each year with their partner. **True**

Fact: *The peacock's colorful tail feathers are used to attract mates.*

Male peacocks display their vibrant tail feathers in a fan to attract females. The size and color of the feathers play a significant role in mating success. **True**

2.3 Reptile Wonders

Dive into the world of reptiles, where you'll meet the ancient crocodiles, sneaky snakes, and resilient tortoises. Learn about their cold-blooded nature, scales, and fascinating survival skills, including how some can regrow lost tails.

Fact: *All reptiles are cold-blooded.*

Reptiles are ectothermic, or cold-blooded, meaning they rely on external sources to regulate their body temperature. They bask in the sun to warm up and seek shade to cool down. **True**

Fact: *Snakes dislocate their jaws to swallow large prey.*

Snakes have highly flexible jaws, allowing them to open their mouths wide and consume prey much larger than their head. They don't dislocate their jaws but instead stretch the ligaments that connect their jawbones. **False**

Fact: *Turtles can leave their shells.*

A turtle's shell is part of its skeleton, made up of fused bones including the spine and rib cage. They cannot leave their shells as it is an integral part of their body. **False**

Fact: *Chameleons change color to blend in with their surroundings.*

Chameleons primarily change color to communicate, regulate their temperature, and respond to emotions, rather than solely for camouflage. However, blending in can be a secondary benefit. **False**

Fact: *Crocodiles can regrow lost teeth.*

Crocodiles can regrow their teeth multiple times throughout their lives. They have a nearly endless supply of replacement teeth, ensuring they always have functional teeth for hunting. **True**

Fact: *Lizards can detach their tails to escape predators.*

Many lizards can voluntarily detach their tails when threatened. This process, called autotomy, allows them to distract predators while they escape. The tail often regrows over time. **True**

Fact: *Some reptiles can live over 100 years.*

Certain reptiles, such as tortoises and some species of turtles, can live over 100 years. The Galápagos tortoise, for example, is known for its exceptional longevity. **True**

Fact: *The Komodo dragon is the largest living lizard.*

The Komodo dragon is the largest living lizard species, capable of growing up to 10 feet in length and weighing over 150 pounds. They are found on a few Indonesian islands. **True**

Fact: *Geckos can walk on walls and ceilings.*

Geckos have specialized toe pads with microscopic hairs that allow them to adhere to and walk on smooth surfaces, including walls and ceilings. **True**

Fact: *Tortoises are the same as turtles.*

Tortoises and turtles are both reptiles but differ in their habitats and physical adaptations. Tortoises are land-dwellers with sturdy, domed shells, while turtles typically live in water and have flatter, more streamlined shells. **False**

Fact: Iguanas can breathe underwater.

Iguanas are not capable of breathing underwater, but some, like the marine iguana, can hold their breath for extended periods while foraging underwater. **False**

Fact: Some reptiles can change their sex.

In some reptile species, like certain turtles and lizards, the temperature at which eggs are incubated can determine the sex of the offspring, effectively changing their sex based on environmental conditions. **True**

Fact: Crocodiles and alligators are the same animals.

Crocodiles and alligators are different species with distinct characteristics. Crocodiles have a V-shaped snout, while alligators have a U-shaped snout. They also differ in behavior and habitat preferences. **False**

Fact: *Reptiles breathe through their skin.*

Unlike amphibians, reptiles cannot breathe through their skin. They rely on lungs to breathe air, which is why they need to surface regularly if they live in water. **False**

Fact: *Some reptiles have a third eye.*

Certain reptiles, like the tuatara and some lizards, have a parietal eye, also known as a third eye. This eye can sense changes in light and helps regulate their biological rhythms. **True**

Fact: *Alligators can climb trees.*

Juvenile alligators and even some adults can climb trees. They often climb to bask in the sun or escape from predators. **True**

Fact: *Chameleons can look in two directions at once.*

Chameleons have unique eyes that can move independently, allowing them to look in two different directions simultaneously. This helps them watch for predators and prey at the same time. **True**

2.4 Marvelous Marine Life

Uncover the mysteries of the deep blue sea, home to incredible creatures like the giant blue whale, playful sea otters, and glowing jellyfish. Discover how marine animals adapt to life underwater, from breathing techniques to bioluminescence.

Fact: *Dolphins are mammals.*

Dolphins are indeed mammals. They are warm-blooded, breathe air through their lungs, give birth to live young and nurse their babies with milk. **True**

Fact: *Sharks are the only fish that can blink.*

Sharks do not have eyelids like humans, but they do have a nictitating membrane that acts like an eyelid to protect their eyes. This makes them unique among fish. **False**

Fact: *Starfish have brains.*

Starfish do not have brains. Instead, they have a complex nervous system that allows them to sense their environment and move. **False**

Fact: *Some jellyfish are immortal.*

Certain species of jellyfish, like the Turritopsis dohrnii, can revert to their juvenile form after reaching adulthood, effectively making them biologically immortal. **True**

Fact: *Octopuses have three hearts.*

Octopuses have three hearts: two pump blood to the gills, and one pumps it to the rest of the body. This unique circulatory system helps them survive in deep waters. **True**

Fact: *All crabs can walk forward.*

Most crabs walk sideways due to the structure of their legs, but some species, like the spider crab, can walk forward and backward. **False**

Fact: *Seahorses are excellent swimmers.*

Seahorses are actually poor swimmers. They use their dorsal fin to propel themselves and rely on their prehensile tails to anchor themselves to seaweed or coral to avoid being swept away by currents. **False**

Fact: *Some fish can fly.*

Flying fish can glide above the water's surface for short distances to escape predators. They achieve this by rapidly beating their tail and using their wing-like pectoral fins. **True**

Fact: Clownfish are immune to jellyfish stings.

Clownfish are immune to the stings of sea anemones, not jellyfish. They have a special mucus on their skin that protects them, allowing them to live among anemones' tentacles. **False**

Fact: Coral reefs are made of rocks.

Coral reefs are formed by colonies of tiny animals called coral polyps. These polyps secrete calcium carbonate, which builds up to form the reef structure over time. **False**

Fact: The Great Barrier Reef is visible from space.

The Great Barrier Reef, the world's largest coral reef system, is so vast that it can be seen from space. It stretches over 1,400 miles off the coast of Australia. **True**

Fact: Male seahorses give birth.

Male seahorses have a specialized pouch where females deposit their eggs. The males then fertilize and carry the eggs until they hatch, giving birth to live young. **True**

Fact: Some squids can produce their own light.

Certain species of squid have bioluminescent organs that allow them to produce light. This ability helps them in camouflage, communication, and attracting prey. **True**

Fact: Electric eels can generate electricity.

Electric eels can generate powerful electric shocks of up to 600 volts, which they use for hunting prey, self-defense, and navigating through murky waters. **True**

Fact: *All marine mammals need to come to the surface to breathe.*

Marine mammals, such as whales, dolphins, and seals, need to surface to breathe air, as they have lungs and cannot extract oxygen from the water. **True**

Fact: *Sea turtles can live up to 200 years.*

While some sea turtles can live a long time, usually around 50 to 100 years, there is no evidence to support that they can live up to 200 years. **False**

Fact: *Starfish can regenerate lost arms.*

Starfish have remarkable regenerative abilities. They can regrow lost arms, and in some cases, an entire starfish can regenerate from a single arm if part of the central disc is attached. **True**

Fact: *Pufferfish can inflate to twice their size.*

Pufferfish can inflate themselves to several times their normal size as a defense mechanism to scare away predators. They ingest water (or air) to puff up. **True**

2.5 Incredible Insects

Step into the miniature world of insects, where tiny creatures like ants, butterflies, and beetles perform extraordinary feats. Learn about their complex societies, metamorphosis, and their crucial role in ecosystems.

Fact: *All insects have six legs.*

Insects belong to the class Insecta and are characterized by having three pairs of legs, totaling six legs. This is a key feature that distinguishes them from other arthropods. **True**

Fact: *Butterflies taste with their feet.*

Butterflies have taste sensors on their feet, allowing them to taste and identify plants by landing on them. This helps them find suitable plants for laying their eggs. **True**

Fact: *All spiders are insects.*

Spiders are not insects; they are arachnids. Arachnids have eight legs and two main body segments, while insects have six legs and three main body segments. **False**

Fact: *All bees live in hives.*

Not all bees live in hives. While honeybees are social and live in hives, many species of bees are solitary and nest in the ground, wood, or other sheltered places. **False**

Fact: *Ants can carry up to 50 times their body weight.*

Ants are incredibly strong for their size, capable of carrying objects up to 50 times their own body weight. This strength helps them gather food and build their nests. **True**

Fact: *Dragonflies can fly backward.*

Dragonflies are skilled fliers with the ability to fly in all directions, including backward. Their two pairs of wings move independently, giving them exceptional maneuverability. **True**

Fact: *Fireflies produce light through bioluminescence.*

Fireflies produce light through a chemical reaction in their bodies called bioluminescence. This light is used to attract mates and communicate with other fireflies. **True**

Fact: *Ladybugs are all female.*

Ladybugs, also known as ladybirds, can be either male or female. Both genders play a role in reproduction and the control of garden pests. **False**

Fact: *Termites are related to cockroaches.*

Termites are closely related to cockroaches. Both belong to the order Blattodea, which includes some of the most ancient insects on Earth. **True**

Fact: *Grasshoppers have ears on their legs.*

Grasshoppers have hearing organs called tympanal organs located on their front legs. These organs help them detect sound vibrations. **True**

Fact: *All insects go through complete metamorphosis.*

Not all insects undergo complete metamorphosis. While butterflies and beetles do, other insects like grasshoppers and dragonflies go through incomplete metamorphosis, which does not include a pupal stage. **False**

Fact: *Insects breathe through their noses.*

Insects do not have noses. They breathe through small openings called spiracles located on the sides of their bodies, which lead to a network of tubes called tracheae. **False**

Fact: *Mosquitoes are the deadliest animals on Earth.*

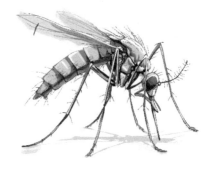

Mosquitoes are considered the deadliest animals because they transmit diseases like malaria, dengue fever, and Zika virus, which cause millions of deaths each year. **True**

Fact: *Bees die after they sting.*

Only worker honeybees die after they sting. Their barbed stingers get stuck in the skin, causing the bee to perish. Other bees and wasps can sting multiple times without dying. **True**

Fact: *Insects have blue blood.*

Insects have hemolymph, which is usually green or yellow, not blue. Hemolymph functions similarly to blood in vertebrates, but it does not carry oxygen. **False**

Fact: *Butterflies have skeletons inside their bodies.*

Butterflies, like all insects, have exoskeletons. Their hard outer shells provide structure and protection, unlike vertebrates with internal skeletons. **False**

Fact: *Cockroaches can live without their heads for weeks.*

Cockroaches can survive for a week or more without their heads because they breathe through spiracles and do not rely on their heads for vital functions like humans do. However, they eventually die from dehydration. **True**

Fact: *Crickets chirp to attract mates.*

Male crickets chirp by rubbing their wings together to attract female mates. The sound is produced by a process called stridulation. **True**

2.6 Amphibian Adventures

Explore the dual life of amphibians, such as frogs, salamanders, and newts, who live both in water and on land. Understand their life cycles, from tadpoles to adults, and how they breathe through their skin and lungs.

Fact: *All amphibians have slimy skin.*

Amphibians have moist skin that is often slimy due to mucus secretion, which helps keep their skin hydrated and aids in respiration. **True**

Fact: *Frogs can only live in water.*

Frogs are amphibians, meaning they can live both in water and on land. They typically start their life in water as tadpoles and then move to land as adults. **False**

Fact: *Frogs use their eyes to help them swallow food.*

Frogs retract their eyes into their heads to help push food down their throats. This unique adaptation assists in the swallowing process. **True**

Fact: *All toads are poisonous.*

Not all toads are poisonous, but many species have glands that produce toxins to deter predators. These toxins can cause irritation or harm if ingested. **False**

Fact: Salamanders can regenerate lost limbs.

Salamanders have the remarkable ability to regenerate lost limbs, tails, and even parts of their

organs, making them unique among amphibians. **True**

Fact: Amphibians can breathe through their skin.

Many amphibians can breathe through their skin, a process known as cutaneous respiration. This is especially important when they are underwater or in moist environments. **True**

Fact: Amphibians are cold-blooded.

Amphibians are ectothermic, or cold-blooded, meaning their body temperature is regulated by their surroundings. **True**

Fact: Toads can give you warts.

Toads do not cause warts. This is a myth. Warts in humans are caused by viruses, not by contact with toads. **False**

Fact: Frogs can drink through their skin.

Frogs absorb water through their skin instead of drinking it with their mouths. They have a specialized area on their belly called the "drinking patch" for this purpose. **True**

Fact: *Some amphibians can freeze and thaw without dying.*

Certain amphibians, like the wood frog, can survive being frozen during the winter and thaw out in the spring, continuing their normal activities. **True**

Fact: *The largest amphibian is the Chinese giant salamander.*

The Chinese giant salamander is the largest amphibian, growing up to 6 feet in length. It is an endangered species found in freshwater habitats in China. **True**

Fact: *Frogs can change color.*

Some frog species can change color to blend in with their environment, communicate with other frogs, or regulate their body temperature. **True**

2.7 Extraordinary Endangered Species

Learn about the amazing animals that are currently endangered and the efforts being made to save them. From the majestic Siberian tiger to the elusive vaquita porpoise, understand the challenges they face and how we can help protect them.

Fact: *The giant panda is no longer endangered.*

Giant pandas have been reclassified from "endangered" to "vulnerable" thanks to extensive conservation efforts, although they are still at risk. **True**

Fact: *All species of sea turtles are endangered.*

While not all sea turtle species are classified as endangered, many, such as the leatherback and hawksbill turtles, are critically endangered. **False**

Fact: *The Amur leopard is one of the rarest big cats in the world.*

With fewer than 100 individuals left in the wild, the Amur leopard is critically endangered and one of the rarest big cats. **True**

Fact: *The bald eagle was once endangered.*

The bald eagle was once endangered in the United States but has since recovered due to conservation efforts and is now listed as "least concern." **True**

Fact: *The black-footed ferret was once considered extinct in the wild.*

The black-footed ferret was thought to be extinct in the wild until a small population was discovered in the 1980s.

Conservation programs have helped increase their numbers. **True**

Fact: *The mountain gorilla population is increasing.*

The mountain gorilla population has been increasing thanks to intensive conservation efforts, but they remain endangered. **True**

Fact: *Polar bears are endangered due to climate change.*

Polar bears are classified as vulnerable, not endangered, but their populations are at serious risk due to the loss of sea ice habitat from climate change. **False**

Fact: *The dodo bird is still alive.*

The dodo bird went extinct in the 17th century due to overhunting and humans' introduction of invasive species. **False**

Fact: *All species of coral reefs are endangered.*

Coral reefs as ecosystems are under threat, but not all species of corals are classified as endangered. Many are, however, at risk due to climate change and pollution. **False**

Fact: *The vaquita is the most endangered marine mammal.*

The vaquita, a small porpoise found in the Gulf of California, is critically endangered with fewer than 20 individuals remaining. **True**

Fact: *The California condor has been saved from extinction.*

The California condor was brought back from the brink of extinction through captive breeding programs, but it remains critically endangered. **True**

Fact: The Tasmanian tiger was recently discovered to be alive.

The Tasmanian tiger, or thylacine, was declared extinct in the 20th century, and there have been no confirmed

sightings since. **False**

Fact: *Bluefin tuna are endangered due to overfishing.*

Bluefin tuna are overfished and considered critically endangered due to high demand for their meat, particularly in sushi and sashimi dishes. **True**

Fact: *The passenger pigeon was saved from extinction.*

The passenger pigeon went extinct in the early 20th century due to excessive hunting and habitat destruction. **False**

2.8: Mythical Creatures and Animal Legends

Explore the fascinating myths and legends surrounding animals from different cultures. From dragons and unicorns to the stories of Anansi the spider and the Native American tales of the trickster coyote, discover how animals have inspired imagination and storytelling throughout history.

Fact: *Unicorns are legendary creatures known for their single horn.*

Unicorns are mythical creatures that have been described in folklore as having a single, spiraled horn on their forehead. They are often depicted as pure. **True**

Fact: *The Loch Ness Monster is a dinosaur.*

The Loch Ness Monster, affectionately known as "Nessie," is a creature from Scottish folklore. Some theories suggest it might be a dinosaur-like creature, but there is no scientific evidence to support this claim. **False**

Fact: *The phoenix is a bird that never dies.*

The phoenix is a mythical bird that is said to live for centuries before burning itself to ashes and then being reborn from those ashes, symbolizing immortality and renewal. **True**

Fact: *Werewolves transform during a full moon.*

Werewolves are legendary creatures believed to transform from human to wolf during a full moon. This transformation is a common theme in folklore and popular culture. **True**

Fact: *Bigfoot is believed to be an alien.*

Bigfoot, also known as Sasquatch, is a legendary ape-like creature from North American folklore. While some fringe theories suggest an alien connection, most stories describe it as an elusive primate. **False**

Fact: *The Minotaur is a creature with the body of a lion and the head of an eagle.*

The Minotaur is actually a creature from Greek mythology with the body of a man and the head of a bull. It lived in the Labyrinth on the island of Crete. **False**

Fact: *The Kraken is a mythical sea monster believed to inhabit the oceans near Norway and Greenland.*

The Kraken is a legendary sea monster from Scandinavian folklore, often described as a giant octopus or squid capable of dragging ships into the depths. **True**

Fact: *Griffins have the body of a lion and the wings and head of an eagle.*

Griffins are mythical creatures with the body of a lion and the wings and head of an eagle. They are often depicted as powerful and majestic guardians. **True**

Fact: *The Chupacabra is a mythical bird known for its beautiful songs.*

The Chupacabra is actually a legendary creature from Latin American folklore, described as a reptilian or dog-like being that attacks livestock, particularly goats. **False**

Fact: *The Cyclops is a giant with a single eye in the middle of its forehead.*

The Cyclops is a mythical giant from Greek mythology, distinguished by having a single eye in the middle of its forehead. They are often depicted as strong but not very intelligent. **True**

Fact: *The Hydra is a mythical creature with a single head.*

The Hydra is a multi-headed serpent from Greek

mythology. When one head is cut off, it is said to grow two more in its place. **False**

Fact: *The Sphinx is a creature with the body of a lion and the head of a pharaoh.*

The Sphinx is a mythical creature from Egyptian mythology with the body of a lion and the head of a human, often a pharaoh. It is known for its enigmatic and imposing presence. **True**

Fact: *Pegasus is a winged wolf from Greek mythology.*

Pegasus is a winged horse from Greek mythology, known for its ability to fly and its association with the hero Bellerophon. **False**

Fact: *The Yeti is a legendary creature said to inhabit the Arctic tundra.*

The Yeti, also known as the Abominable Snowman, is a mythical creature believed to inhabit the Himalayan mountains, not the Arctic tundra. **False**

Fact: *The Thunderbird is a creature from Native American mythology known for creating storms.*

The Thunderbird is a powerful and mythical bird from Native American mythology, believed to create thunder and lightning with the beating of its wings. **True**

Fact: *The Cerberus is a three-headed dog that guards the underworld in Greek mythology.*

Cerberus is a mythical three-headed dog from Greek mythology that guards the entrance to the underworld, preventing the dead from leaving and the living from entering. **True**

CHAPTER 3: WONDERS OF THE HUMAN BODY

3.1 The Amazing Brain

Did you know that your brain generates enough electricity to power a small light bulb?

Fact: *Your brain is the fattiest organ in your body.*

The human brain is composed of approximately 60% fat, making it the fattiest organ in your body. This fat is crucial for protecting nerve cells and ensuring efficient communication within the brain. **True**

Fact: *The brain stops developing after childhood.*

The brain continues to develop and change throughout your entire life. While significant development happens during childhood, the brain remains adaptable and capable of forming new connections well into adulthood. **False**

Fact: *Humans use only 10% of their brains.*

The myth that humans use only 10% of their brains has been debunked. Brain imaging technology shows that we use virtually every part of the brain, and most of it is active almost all the time. **False**

Fact: *Your brain generates enough electricity to power a light bulb.*

The human brain produces about 20 watts of electrical power, enough to power a small light bulb. This electrical activity is crucial for sending signals throughout your body. **True**

Fact: The brain can feel pain.

The brain itself does not have pain receptors and cannot feel pain. This is why brain surgery can be performed on a patient while they are awake. However, the brain can process pain signals from other parts of the body. **False**

Fact: Your brain is fully grown by the age of 18.

While the brain reaches about 90% of its adult size by age 6, it continues to mature and develop well into your mid-20s, particularly the frontal lobes, which are responsible for decision-making and self-control. **False**

Fact: Each side of the brain controls the opposite side of the body.

The left hemisphere of the brain controls the right side of the body, and the right hemisphere controls the left side. This is known as contralateral control. **True**

Fact: *Your brain's storage capacity is virtually unlimited.*

The human brain has an astonishing capacity for storage. Estimates suggest that it can hold around 2.5 petabytes of information, which is roughly equivalent to 3 million hours of TV shows. **True**

Fact: *Memories are stored in one specific area of the brain.*

Memories are not stored in just one area of the brain. Instead, they are distributed across various regions, with different types of memories (such as procedural or episodic) involving different networks of brain cells. **False**

Fact: *The brain is more active at night than during the day.*

During sleep, the brain remains highly active, engaging in processes such as memory consolidation and problem-solving. Certain stages of sleep involve intense brain activity, making the brain sometimes more active at night than during the day. **True**

3.2 The Beating Heart

Heart Facts: Discover interesting facts about heart rates, heart sizes, and how the heart keeps you alive.

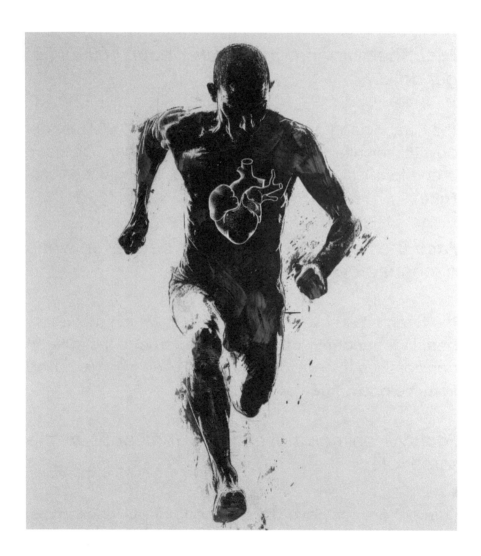

Fact: *Your heart is about the size of your fist.*

The size of your heart is roughly equivalent to the size of your own fist. This amazing organ is powerful enough to pump blood throughout your entire body. **True**

Fact: *The human heart beats about 1,000 times per day.*

The human heart actually beats around 100,000 times per day. This relentless beating ensures that oxygen-rich blood is constantly circulating to keep your body functioning. **False**

Fact: *The heart can continue to beat even when disconnected from the body.*

The heart has its own electrical system, which allows it to beat independently of the brain. Because of this, a heart can continue to beat for a short time even when removed from the body. **True**

Fact: *All animals have hearts that beat at the same rate.*

Different animals have different heart rates. For example, a mouse's heart can beat up to 500 times per minute, while an elephant's heart beats around 25 times per minute. **False**

Fact: *The heart pumps about 2,000 gallons of blood each day.*

Your heart works incredibly hard, pumping around 2,000 gallons of blood through your body each day. This blood travels through a vast network of blood vessels, ensuring that every part of your body receives oxygen and nutrients. **True**

Fact: *The sound of a heartbeat is caused by the heart valve opening.*

The sound of a heartbeat is actually caused by the closing of the heart valves. These valves ensure that blood flows in the correct direction through the heart's chambers. **False**

Fact: *Your heart is located in the center of your chest.*

While many people think the heart is located on the left side, it is situated in the center of the chest, slightly tilted to the left. **True**

Fact: *Exercise makes your heart weaker because it has to work harder.*

Exercise strengthens your heart, making it more efficient at pumping blood. Regular physical activity can improve heart health and lower the risk of heart disease. **False**

Fact: *Eating a lot of junk food is good for your heart.*

Eating a diet high in junk food can increase the risk of heart disease. A heart-healthy diet includes fruits, vegetables, whole grains, and lean proteins. **False**

Fact: *The human heart has four chambers.*

The human heart has four chambers: two atria (upper chambers) and two ventricles (lower chambers). These chambers work together to pump blood throughout the body. **True**

Fact: *Blood in your veins is blue.*

Blood is always red, although it appears blue when viewed through the skin. Oxygen-rich blood is bright red, while oxygen-poor blood is a darker red. **False**

Fact: *The heart rate of a baby is slower than that of an adult.*

A baby's heart rate is much faster than an adult's. Newborns can have heart rates of 120-160 beats per minute, while an average adult's heart rate is 60-100 beats per minute. **False**

3.3 Super Skeleton

Bone Facts: Did you know that humans have over 200 bones? Find out more about how bones grow and change.

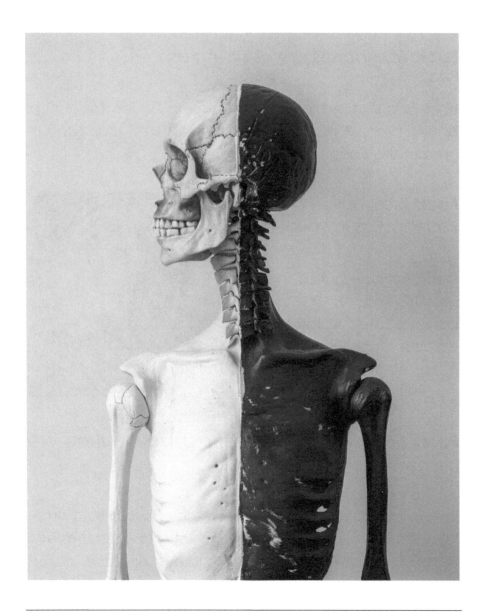

Fact: *The human skeleton is made up of over 500 bones.*

The human skeleton is composed of 206 bones in adulthood. At birth, we have around 270 bones, but some of them fuse together as we grow. **False**

Fact: *Your bones are as strong as steel.*

Bone is an incredibly strong material. Ounce for ounce, bone is stronger than steel, capable of withstanding forces greater than concrete. **True**

Fact: *The smallest bone in your body is in your ear.*

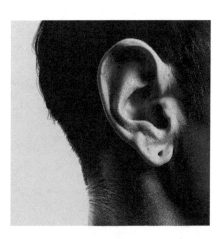

The smallest bone in the human body is the stapes bone, located in the middle ear. It is roughly the size of a grain of rice and plays a crucial role in hearing. **True**

Fact: *Bones are lightweight because they are hollow.*

Bones are not completely hollow; they have a solid outer layer called the cortical bone, which provides strength. Inside, bones have a spongy, porous structure called trabecular bone, which makes them lightweight and flexible. **True**

Fact: *All bones are hard and brittle.*

Bones are hard but not brittle. They are made of a combination of collagen (which provides flexibility) and calcium phosphate (which provides strength), allowing them to be both sturdy and slightly flexible. **False**

Fact: *You stop growing new bone tissue after you turn 20.*

Bone remodeling, the process of creating new bone tissue, continues throughout your life. However, the balance between new bone formation and old bone removal changes with age. **False**

Fact: *The femur is the longest bone in the human body.*

The femur, or thigh bone, is the longest and strongest bone in the human body. It supports the weight of the body and allows for a range of movements. **True**

Fact: *Your skeleton makes up about half of your body weight.*

The skeleton accounts for approximately 14-20% of a person's total body weight. The majority of body weight comes from muscles, organs, and other tissues. **False**

Fact: *The skull is made up of one solid bone.*

The skull is composed of 22 bones that are fused together. These include the cranial bones that protect the brain and the facial bones that form the structure of the face. **False**

Fact: *Your bones produce blood cells.*

Bone marrow, found in the hollow parts of certain bones, produces red blood cells, white blood cells, and platelets. This process is known as hematopoiesis. **True**

Fact: *Joints are where two bones meet and move.*

Joints are the locations where two or more bones meet. They allow for movement and flexibility, with different types of joints providing different ranges of motion. **True**

Fact: *Teeth are considered bones.*

Teeth are not bones. Although they are similar in some ways, teeth are made of enamel and dentin, which are harder and denser than bone. **False**

3.4. Mighty Muscles

Muscle Facts: Learn about the different types of muscles and how they help us move and function.

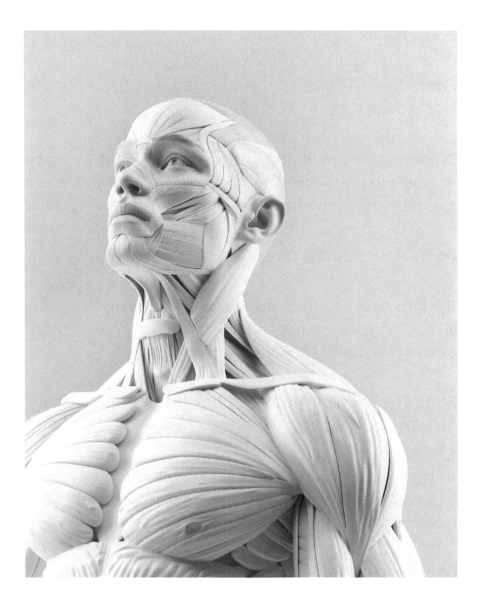

Fact: *There are over 1,000 muscles in the human body.*

The human body has approximately 600 muscles. These muscles are essential for movement, stability, and various bodily functions. **False**

Fact: *The tongue is the strongest muscle in the body.*

The tongue is very strong and versatile, but the strongest muscle in terms of exerting force is the masseter, the jaw muscle. It can generate great pressure for chewing. **False**

Fact: *Your heart is a muscle.*

The heart is a muscular organ known as the myocardium. It continuously pumps blood throughout your body, working tirelessly without rest. **True**

Fact: *The largest muscle in the body is the gluteus maximus.*

The gluteus maximus, located in the buttocks, is the largest muscle in the body. It is responsible for movement of the hip and thigh. **True**

Fact: *You have muscles in your fingers.*

There are no muscles in your fingers themselves. The muscles that control finger movements are located in the palm and forearm and are connected to the fingers by tendons. **False**

Fact: *Smiling uses more muscles than frowning.*

Smiling uses fewer muscles than frowning. It takes about 17 muscles to smile and 43 muscles to frown. So, it's easier to smile than to frown! **False**

Fact: *Muscles are only found in your arms and legs.*

Muscles are found throughout your body, including your torso, face, and even inside organs like the heart and stomach. They are essential for all types of movement and functions. **False**

Fact: *The diaphragm is a muscle that helps you breathe.*

The diaphragm is a dome-shaped muscle located below the lungs. It contracts and flattens when you inhale, allowing your lungs to expand and fill with air. **True**

Fact: Exercise makes muscles grow stronger.

When you exercise, especially through strength training, you create tiny tears in your muscle fibers. As these fibers repair, they grow stronger and larger. **True**

Fact: All muscles are under voluntary control.

Not all muscles are under voluntary control. Skeletal muscles are controlled voluntarily, while smooth muscles (like those in your digestive system) and cardiac muscles (heart) function involuntarily. **False**

Fact: Muscle memory helps you perform repeated tasks more efficiently.

Muscle memory refers to the process by which muscles become accustomed to performing tasks through repetition, allowing you to perform them more efficiently over time. **True**

3.5 Dynamic Digestive System

Digestive Facts: Discover amazing facts about digestion, like how long it takes for food to digest.

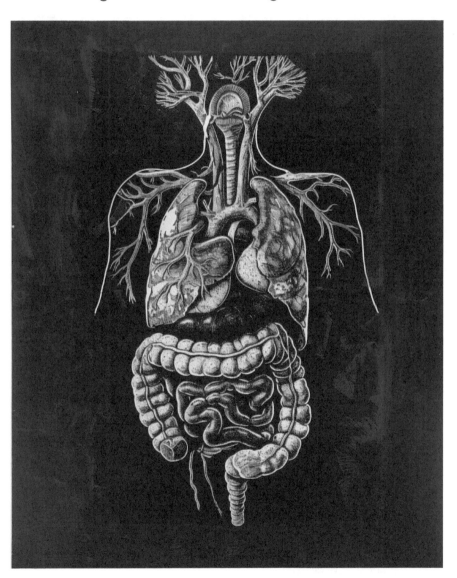

Fact: *Digestion starts in the stomach.*

Digestion actually begins in the mouth. When you chew your food, enzymes in your saliva start breaking down the food, beginning the digestive process before it reaches the stomach. **False**

Fact: *The small intestine is shorter than the large intestine.*

Despite its name, the small intestine is much longer than the large intestine. The small intestine is about 20 feet long, while the large intestine is about 5 feet long. **False**

Fact: *Your stomach only digests food when you're awake.*

Your stomach continues to digest food whether you are awake or asleep. Digestion is an automatic process that works around the clock. **False**

Fact: *The liver produces bile, which helps digest fats.*

The liver produces bile, a substance that helps break down fats into smaller molecules that can be absorbed by the body. Bile is stored in the gallbladder and released into the small intestine. **True**

Fact: *The digestive system is also known as the alimentary canal.*

The digestive system, also known as the alimentary canal, is a continuous tube that runs from the mouth to the anus, processing food into energy and nutrients the body can use. **True**

Fact: *You have more than one stomach.*

Humans have only one stomach. However, some animals, like cows, have multiple stomach compartments to aid in digesting tough plant materials. **False**

Fact: *It takes about 24-72 hours for food to pass through the digestive system.*

The entire digestive process can take anywhere from 24 to 72 hours, depending on the type of food consumed and the individual's digestive health. **True**

Fact: *The appendix is a vital organ in digestion.*

The appendix is not considered a vital organ for digestion. It is a small, tube-like structure attached to the large intestine. Its exact purpose is still not fully understood, though it may play a role in the immune system. **False**

Fact: *The stomach is protected from its own acid by a layer of mucus.*

The stomach lining is protected by a thick layer of mucus that prevents the strong stomach acids from damaging the stomach walls. **True**

Fact: *Most nutrient absorption happens in the stomach.*

Most nutrient absorption occurs in the small intestine. The walls of the small intestine have many folds and villi that increase the surface area for absorbing nutrients from digested food. **False**

Fact: *The pancreas produces enzymes that aid in digestion.*

The pancreas produces enzymes that help digest proteins, fats, and carbohydrates in the small intestine. It also releases insulin to help regulate blood sugar levels. **True**

Fact: *Chewing food thoroughly aids digestion.*

Chewing food thoroughly breaks it down into smaller pieces, making it easier for enzymes to digest it. This helps ensure better nutrient absorption and overall digestion. **True**

3.6 Brilliant Blood and Circulation

Blood Facts: Learn interesting facts about blood types, blood cells, and how much blood is in your body.

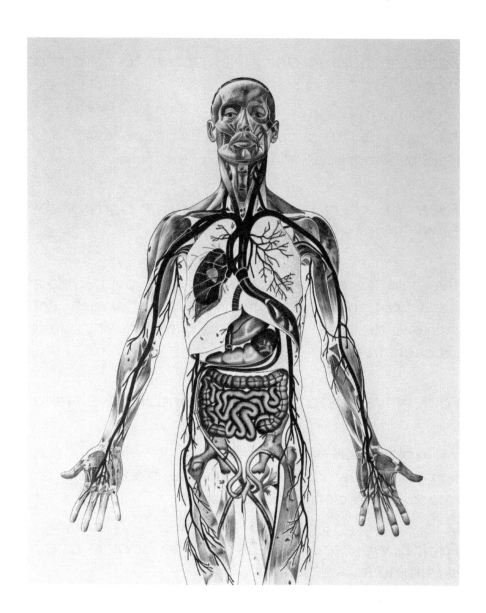

Fact: *Blood is always red.*

Blood is always red due to the iron in hemoglobin, which binds to oxygen. Oxygen-rich blood is bright red, while oxygen-poor blood is a darker red. **True**

Fact: *The human body has about 10 gallons of blood.*

The human body has about 1.2 to 1.5 gallons (or 4.5 to 5.5 liters) of blood, depending on body size. **False**

Fact: *The heart pumps blood to all parts of the body.*

The heart is a powerful muscle that pumps blood throughout the entire body, delivering oxygen and nutrients to tissues and organs and removing waste products. **True**

Fact: *White blood cells are responsible for clotting.*

White blood cells are part of the immune system and help fight infections. Platelets, not white blood cells, are responsible for clotting blood. **False**

Fact: *Blood circulates through the body in about one minute.*

Blood takes approximately one minute to make a full circuit through the body, traveling through the heart, lungs, and various tissues. **True**

Fact: *The circulatory system includes the heart, blood vessels, and lungs.*

The circulatory system consists of the heart, blood vessels (arteries, veins, and capillaries), and blood. The lungs are part of the respiratory system but work closely with the circulatory system to exchange gases. **False**

Fact: *Arteries carry blood away from the heart.*

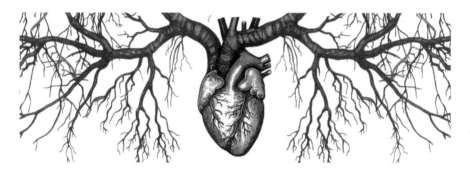

Arteries are blood vessels that carry oxygen-rich blood away from the heart to the rest of the body. Veins return oxygen-poor blood back to the heart. **True**

Fact: *Capillaries are the largest blood vessels in the body.*

Capillaries are the smallest blood vessels in the body. They connect arteries and veins and facilitate the exchange of

oxygen, nutrients, and waste between blood and tissues.
False

Fact: *Red blood cells live for about 120 days.*

Red blood cells have a lifespan of about 120 days. After this period, they are broken down and recycled by the body. **True**

Fact: *The heart has two chambers.*

The heart has four chambers: two upper chambers called atria and two lower chambers called ventricles. These chambers work together to pump blood throughout the body. **False**

Fact: *Blood makes up about 8% of your body weight.*

Blood accounts for approximately 8% of a person's body weight, playing a crucial role in maintaining bodily functions. **True**

Fact: *The aorta is the smallest artery in the body.*

The aorta is actually the largest artery in the body. It carries oxygen-rich blood from the heart to the rest of the body. **False**

3.7 Sensational Senses

The Five Senses: Discover how sight, hearing, taste, touch, and smell work together to help us experience the world.

Fact: *Humans have more than five senses.*

While we commonly refer to the five senses (sight, hearing, taste, smell, and touch), humans actually have more, including balance (vestibular sense), temperature (thermoception), and body position (proprioception). **True**

Fact: *Your eyes can see in total darkness.*

Eyes need light to see. In complete darkness, it's impossible to see because there is no light for the eyes to detect and process. **False**

Fact: *The tongue has different regions for each taste.*

The idea that different regions of the tongue detect different tastes (sweet, sour, salty, bitter, and umami) is a myth. All taste buds can detect all types of tastes. **False**

Fact: *Your sense of smell is strongest when you are a child.*

The sense of smell is typically strongest during childhood and tends to diminish with age. Children have a more acute sense of smell than adults. **True**

Fact: *Ears not only help you hear but also help you balance.*

The inner ear contains the vestibular system, which helps control balance and spatial orientation. This system works with your eyes and muscles to keep you balanced. **True**

Fact: *Humans can distinguish over a million different colors.*

The human eye can distinguish about 10 million different colors, thanks to the cone cells in our retinas that detect various wavelengths of light. **True**

Fact: *Your sense of touch is the same all over your body.*

The sense of touch varies in sensitivity across different parts of the body. Fingertips and lips are much more sensitive to touch than areas like your back. **False**

Fact: *Your nose can remember 50,000 different scents.*

The human nose is capable of remembering and distinguishing about 50,000 different scents, showcasing the incredible capacity of our olfactory system. **True**

Fact: *The sense of hearing can regenerate if damaged.*

Unlike some animals, humans cannot regenerate the hair cells in the inner ear once they are damaged. Hearing loss from damaged hair cells is usually permanent. **False**

Fact: *Reading in dim light can damage your eyes.*

Reading in dim light does not damage your eyes, but it can cause eye strain and temporary discomfort. **False**

Fact: *The brain interprets all sensory information.*

All sensory information (sight, sound, taste, smell, and touch) is processed and interpreted by the brain, allowing us to understand and interact with our environment. **True**

Fact: *Some people can hear colors and see sounds.*

This rare condition is called synesthesia, where one or more additional senses simultaneously perceive one sense. For example, individuals might associate colors with specific sounds. **True**

Fact: *Dogs have a better sense of taste than humans.*

Dogs actually have fewer taste buds than humans—about 1,700 compared to our 9,000. However, dogs rely more on their powerful sense of smell to experience flavors. **False**

Fact: *You can taste food better when you hold your nose.*

Smell significantly enhances the flavor of food. Holding your nose while eating can make food taste bland because you lose the added sensory input from your olfactory system. **True**

Fact: *Your eyes are always the same size from birth.*

Human eyes grow slightly after birth but reach their full size relatively early in life. They remain about the same size from childhood through adulthood. **True**

3.8 Skin: The Body's Largest Organ

Skin Facts: Did you know your skin renews itself every 28 days? Find out more cool facts about your skin.

Fact: *Your skin is the heaviest organ in your body.*

The skin is indeed the heaviest organ, making up about 16% of your total body weight. It acts as a protective barrier and helps regulate body temperature. **True**

Fact: *Your skin regenerates every 28-30 days.*

The outer layer of your skin, the epidermis, constantly sheds dead cells and replaces them with new ones, completing a full cycle approximately every month. **True**

Fact: *The thickest skin on your body is on your palms and soles.*

The skin on your palms and the soles of your feet is the thickest, designed to handle friction and pressure, while the thinnest skin is on your eyelids. **True**

Fact: *Your skin stops growing when you become an adult.*

Your skin continuously regenerates and can grow and stretch throughout your life. This is especially evident during growth spurts in childhood and adolescence, and also when the skin stretches during pregnancy. **False**

Fact: *Your skin has three main layers.*

Your skin is composed of three main layers: the epidermis (outer layer), dermis (middle layer), and hypodermis (inner layer). Each layer has specific functions, from protection to temperature regulation. **True**

Fact: *Your skin can change color in response to emotions.*

Your skin can change color due to emotional responses. For example, you might turn red when you're embarrassed or pale when you're scared. This happens due to changes in blood flow. **True**

Fact: *Your fingerprints are unique and never change.*

Everyone's fingerprints are unique and remain unchanged throughout their lives. Even identical twins have different fingerprints. **True**

Fact: *Skin is waterproof.*

Your skin acts as a waterproof barrier, preventing excessive water loss from the body and protecting against external water entering the body. **True**

Fact: *The skin on your lips is different from the skin on the rest of your body.*

The skin on your lips is much thinner and has fewer layers than the rest of your skin, making them more sensitive and prone to chapping. **True**

Fact: *Your skin can only produce sweat when you exercise.*

Your skin produces sweat not only during exercise but also to regulate body temperature in hot conditions or when you're nervous. **False**

Fact: *Everyone has the same number of melanocytes, the cells that produce melanin.*

While everyone has a similar number of melanocytes, the amount of melanin produced by these cells varies, leading to different skin tones. **True**

Fact: *Goosebumps are a way for your skin to keep you warm.*
Goosebumps occur when tiny muscles at the base of hair follicles contract, causing the hair to stand up. This reaction is a vestige from our ancestors, whose body hair would trap heat to keep them warm. **True**

CHAPTER 4: MYSTERIES OF SPACE

4.1 The Solar System

Fun Facts About Planets: Discover interesting facts about each planet, like which one has the most moons and which is the hottest.

Fact: *The Sun is a star.*

The Sun is indeed a star, a massive ball of hot gas primarily composed of hydrogen and helium. It provides the light and heat necessary for life on Earth. **True**

Fact: *Mercury is the hottest planet in the solar system.*

Despite being closest to the Sun, Mercury is not the hottest planet. Venus holds that title due to its thick atmosphere that traps heat. **False**

Fact: *Earth is the only planet with water.*

Earth is the only known planet with liquid water on its surface. However, scientists have found evidence of ice and possibly liquid water beneath the surface of moons like Europa and Enceladus. **False**

Fact: *Jupiter has the shortest day of all the planets.*

Jupiter has the shortest day in the solar system, taking just under 10 hours to complete a full rotation on its axis. **True**

Fact: *Saturn is the only planet with rings.*

While Saturn is famous for its spectacular rings, it is not the only planet with rings. Jupiter, Uranus, and Neptune also have ring systems, though they are less prominent. **False**

Fact: *Mars is often called the "Red Planet."*

Mars is known as the "Red Planet" because of its reddish appearance, which is due to iron oxide, or rust, on its surface. **True**

Fact: *Venus rotates in the same direction as Earth.*

Venus rotates in the opposite direction to most planets, including Earth. This means the Sun rises in the west and sets in the east on Venus. **False**

Fact: *The Great Red Spot on Jupiter is a giant storm.*

The Great Red Spot is a massive storm on Jupiter that has been raging for at least 400 years. It is so large that three Earths could fit inside it. **True**

Fact: *Neptune is the farthest planet from the Sun.*

Neptune is the eighth and farthest known planet from the Sun in our solar system. **True**

Fact: *Pluto is still classified as a planet.*

Pluto was reclassified as a "dwarf planet" in 2006 by the International Astronomical Union. It is no longer considered one of the main planets in the solar system. **False**

Fact: *Uranus is tilted on its side.*

Uranus has an extreme axial tilt of about 98 degrees, causing it to rotate on its side. This unique tilt gives Uranus extreme seasons. **True**

Fact: *The Sun makes up 99% of the mass of the solar system.*

The Sun accounts for about 99.86% of the total mass of the solar system, dominating its gravitational field and holding the planets in orbit. **True**

Fact: *Mars has the tallest volcano in the solar system.*

Olympus Mons on Mars is the tallest volcano and the largest shield volcano in the solar system, standing about 13.6 miles (22 kilometers) high. **True**

Fact: *There are more than 200 moons in our solar system.*

Over 200 known moons are orbiting the planets in our solar system, with many of them orbiting the gas giants Jupiter and Saturn. **True**

Fact: *A year on Neptune is longer than a year on Earth.*

A year on Neptune, the time it takes to orbit the Sun, is about 165 Earth years. **True**

4.2 Stars and Constellations

What Are Stars?: Learn about the life cycle of stars, from their birth in nebulas to their various end stages like supernovas or black holes.

Fact: *Stars are all the same color.*

Stars come in a variety of colors, including red, yellow, white, and blue. The color of a star is determined by its temperature, with blue stars being the hottest and red stars being the coolest. **False**

Fact: *Constellations look the same from anywhere in the universe.*

Constellations are patterns of stars that appear from our perspective on Earth. If you were on another planet or in another part of the universe, the stars would look different, and the familiar constellations would not be the same. **False**

Fact: *The North Star, Polaris, is the brightest star in the night sky.*

Polaris, the North Star, is not the brightest star in the night sky. The brightest star is actually Sirius, also known as the Dog Star, which is part of the constellation Canis Major. **False**

Fact: *Stars live forever.*

Stars have life cycles. They are born in nebulae, live for millions or billions of years, and eventually die. The fate of a star depends on its mass; some end as white dwarfs, others as neutron stars, or even black holes. **False**

Fact: *The constellation Orion is visible from both the Northern and Southern Hemispheres.*

Orion, one of the most recognizable constellations, can be seen from both the Northern and Southern Hemispheres. It is best visible during the winter months in the Northern Hemisphere. **True**

Fact: *All the stars we see in the night sky are in our galaxy.*

All the stars visible to the naked eye from Earth are indeed part of the Milky Way galaxy. Our galaxy contains billions of stars, and those we see form just a tiny fraction of the total. **True**

Fact: *Constellations are used for navigation.*

Constellations, such as the Big Dipper and the Southern Cross, have been used for navigation for centuries. They help travelers find directions by identifying the positions of stars. **True**

Fact: The sun is the largest star in the universe.

The Sun is an average-sized star known as a yellow dwarf. Many stars in the universe are much larger, such as red giants and supergiants. **False**

Fact: Stars twinkle because they are moving.

Stars appear to twinkle because of the Earth's atmosphere. As the light from a star passes through the layers of the atmosphere, it is bent and refracted, making the star's light appear to flicker. **False**

Fact: A supernova is the explosion of a star

A supernova is a powerful explosion that occurs at the end of a star's life cycle. It can outshine an entire galaxy for a short period and leave behind a neutron star or black hole. **True**

Fact: *Black holes are visible in space.*

Black holes themselves are invisible because no light can escape them. However, we can detect black holes by observing the behavior of nearby stars and gas, which emit X-rays as they are pulled towards the black hole. **False**

4.3 The Moon and Its Phases

Moon Facts: Discover fascinating facts about the Moon, including its surface, gravity, and how it affects tides on Earth.

Fact: *The Moon has its own light.*

The Moon does not produce its own light. Instead, it reflects the light from the Sun. The bright light we see from the Moon at night is sunlight bouncing off its surface. **False**

Fact: *The Moon changes shape every night.*

The Moon appears to change shape due to its phases, which are caused by the relative positions of the Earth, Moon, and Sun. These phases cycle through New Moon, Crescent, First Quarter, Gibbous, and Full Moon, but the Moon itself doesn't change shape. **False**

Fact: *A "Blue Moon" is blue in color.*

A "Blue Moon" refers to the occurrence of a second full moon within a single calendar month, not the color of the moon. The moon does not actually turn blue during this event. **False**

Fact: *The same side of the Moon always faces the Earth.*

The Moon is tidally locked with Earth, meaning the same side (the near side) always faces us. The far side of the Moon, often called the "dark side," is never visible from Earth. **True**

Fact: *The Moon's phases affect the tides on Earth.*

The gravitational pull of the Moon affects the Earth's tides. During the Full Moon and New Moon phases, the tides are stronger, resulting in higher high tides and lower low tides, known as spring tides. **True**

Fact: *The Moon is larger than the planet Mercury.*

The Moon is smaller than the planet Mercury. Mercury has a diameter of about 4,880 kilometers, while the Moon's diameter is about 3,474 kilometers. **False**

Fact: *It takes the Moon one week to complete a full cycle of phases.*

The Moon takes about 29.5 days to complete a full cycle of phases, known as a lunar month. This includes all the phases from New Moon to Full Moon and back to New Moon. **False**

Fact: *There is no gravity on the Moon.*

There is gravity on the Moon, but it is much weaker than on Earth. The Moon's gravity is about one-sixth that of Earth's, allowing astronauts to jump higher and carry heavy objects more easily. **False**

Fact: *A lunar eclipse occurs when the Earth is between the Sun and the Moon.*

A lunar eclipse happens when the Earth comes between the Sun and the Moon, causing the Earth's shadow to fall on the Moon. This can result in a total, partial, or penumbral eclipse. **True**

Fact: *The Moon's surface is smooth and flat.*

The Moon's surface is not smooth and flat; it is covered with craters, mountains, and valleys. These features were formed by impacts from meteoroids and volcanic activity. **False**

4.4 Galaxies and the Universe

What is a Galaxy?: Learn about different types of galaxies, including spiral, elliptical, and irregular galaxies.

Fact: *The Milky Way is the only galaxy in the universe.*

The Milky Way is just one of billions of galaxies in the universe. Each galaxy contains millions or even billions of stars, along with gas, dust, and dark matter. **False**

Fact: *Galaxies can collide with each other.*

Galaxies can and do collide with each other. When galaxies collide, they can merge to form a larger galaxy. These collisions can trigger the formation of new stars. **True**

Fact: *Our solar system is located at the center of the Milky Way galaxy.*

Our solar system is located in one of the outer arms of the Milky Way galaxy, not at its center. The center of the Milky Way contains a supermassive black hole. **False**

Fact: *The Andromeda Galaxy is moving away from the Milky Way.*

The Andromeda Galaxy is actually moving towards the Milky Way. It is expected to collide with our galaxy in about

4.5 billion years. **False**

Fact: *Black holes can be found at the centers of most galaxies.*

Most large galaxies, including the Milky Way, have supermassive black holes at their centers. These black holes can have masses millions or even billions of times that of the Sun. **True**

Fact: *The universe has a definite edge.*

The universe does not have a definite edge that we can observe. It is constantly expanding, and the observable universe is limited by the distance that light has traveled since the Big Bang. **False**

Fact: *There are more stars in the universe than grains of sand on all Earth's beaches.*

There are estimated to be more stars in the universe than there are grains of sand on all the beaches on Earth. This highlights the vastness of the cosmos. **True**

Fact: *The universe is about 13.8 billion years old.*

Scientists estimate that the universe is about 13.8 billion years old, based on observations of the cosmic microwave background radiation and the expansion rate of the universe. **True**

Fact: *All galaxies have spiral shapes.*

Galaxies come in a variety of shapes, including spiral, elliptical, and irregular. The Milky Way is a spiral galaxy, but not all galaxies have this shape. **False**

Fact: *The speed of light is the fastest speed in the universe.*

The speed of light, approximately 299,792 kilometers per second (186,282 miles per second), is the fastest speed in the universe. Nothing can travel faster than the speed of light in a vacuum. **True**

4.5 Space Exploration

Space Missions: Learn about famous space missions, including the Apollo missions, Mars rovers, and the International Space Station.

Fact: *The first human to travel into space was Neil Armstrong.*

The first human to travel into space was Yuri Gagarin, a Soviet astronaut, who orbited the Earth on April 12, 1961. An American astronaut, Neil Armstrong was the first to walk on the Moon. **False**

Fact: *The Hubble Space Telescope was launched before the first Moon landing.*

The Hubble Space Telescope was launched on April 24, 1990, many years after the first Moon landing, which occurred on July 20, 1969. **False**

Fact: *Spacecraft can travel faster than the speed of light.*

According to our current understanding of physics, nothing can travel faster than the speed of light. Spacecraft travel much slower, even though they move incredibly fast compared to speeds on Earth. **False**

Fact: *The International Space Station (ISS) orbits Earth about 16 times a day.*

The ISS orbits Earth approximately 16 times each day, traveling at a speed of about 28,000 kilometers per hour (17,500 miles per hour). **True**

Fact: *Only astronauts from the United States have walked on the Moon.*

All twelve astronauts who have walked on the Moon were part of NASA's Apollo missions and were from the United States. **True**

Fact: *The Voyager 1 spacecraft has left our solar system.*

Voyager 1, launched in 1977, has traveled beyond our solar system into interstellar space. It is the farthest human-made object from Earth. **True**

Fact: *Mars is the only planet in our solar system that has been explored by rovers.*

While Mars has been extensively explored by rovers like Curiosity and Perseverance, the Moon has also been explored by rovers. Additionally, Venus and Saturn's moon Titan have been explored by landers. **False**

Fact: *The first artificial satellite to orbit Earth was the Hubble Space Telescope.*

The first artificial satellite to orbit Earth was Sputnik 1, launched by the Soviet Union on October 4, 1957. The Hubble Space Telescope was launched much later, in 1990. **False**

Fact: *Humans have landed on Mars.*

As of now, humans have not yet landed on Mars. Various missions have sent robotic landers and rovers to explore the Martian surface, but human exploration is still in the planning stages. **False**

Fact: *The Apollo missions brought back samples of Moon rocks to Earth.*

The Apollo missions, conducted by NASA, brought back a total of 382 kilograms (842 pounds) of Moon rocks, soil, and core samples to Earth for scientific study. **True**

4.6. Comets, Asteroids, and Meteors

Famous Space Rocks: Discover famous comets like Halley's Comet and significant meteor impacts on Earth.

Fact: *Comets are often called "dirty snowballs."*

Comets are composed of ice, dust, and rocky material, earning them the nickname "dirty snowballs." When they approach the Sun, the heat causes them to release gas and dust, forming a glowing coma and tail. **True**

Fact: *Asteroids are found primarily in the Oort Cloud.*

Asteroids are mainly found in the asteroid belt, which lies between the orbits of Mars and Jupiter. The Oort Cloud is a distant region that is believed to contain many icy bodies, including comets. **False**

Fact: *Meteors are chunks of rock that float in space.*

Meteors are actually the streaks of light we see in the sky when meteoroids (small pieces of rock or metal) enter the Earth's atmosphere and burn up due to friction with the air. **False**

Fact: *A meteorite is a meteoroid that reaches the Earth's surface.*

When a meteoroid survives its passage through the Earth's atmosphere and lands on the Earth's surface, it is called a meteorite. **True**

Fact: *The largest asteroid in our solar system is Vesta.*

The largest asteroid in our solar system is Ceres, which is also classified as a dwarf planet. Vesta is one of the largest asteroids but not the biggest. **False**

Fact: *Halley's Comet is visible from Earth every 76 years.*

Halley's Comet is one of the most famous comets and is visible from Earth approximately every 76 years. The next appearance will be in 2061. **True**

Fact: *Asteroids can have moons.*

Some asteroids have small moons or companion asteroids that orbit them. An example is the asteroid Ida, which has a moon named Dactyl. **True**

Fact: Meteoroids are larger than asteroids.

Meteoroids are generally smaller than asteroids. They are small particles from comets or asteroids, usually less than a meter in diameter. **False**

Fact: The Chicxulub crater in Mexico was formed by a comet impact.

The Chicxulub crater was formed by an asteroid impact about 66 million years ago, which is believed to have caused the mass extinction of the dinosaurs. **False**

Fact: Comet tails always point away from the Sun.

Comet tails always point away from the Sun due to the pressure of the solar wind. As the comet approaches the Sun, its tail extends in the opposite direction. **True**

CHAPTER 5: EARTH AND ENVIRONMENT

5.1 Natural Disasters

Types of Natural Disasters: Learn about different natural disasters, including earthquakes, volcanoes, tsunamis, and floods.

Fact: *Earthquakes can happen on any part of the Earth's surface.*

Earthquakes typically occur along the edges of tectonic plates where the Earth's crust is most active. However, they can also happen away from these boundaries due to faults and other geological activities. **False**

Fact: *A tsunami is a giant tidal wave.*

A tsunami is not a tidal wave but a series of large ocean waves caused by underwater earthquakes, volcanic eruptions, or landslides. These waves can travel at high speeds across the ocean and cause significant damage when they reach land. **False**

Fact: *Tornadoes only occur in the United States.*

While the United States experiences the most tornadoes, especially in "Tornado Alley," tornadoes can occur in many parts of the world, including Europe, Australia, and Asia. **False**

Fact: *Hurricanes are the same as typhoons and cyclones.*

Hurricanes, typhoons, and cyclones are different names for the same type of storm, depending on where they occur. Hurricanes happen in the Atlantic and Northeast Pacific, typhoons in the Northwest Pacific, and cyclones in the South Pacific and Indian Ocean. **True**

Fact: Volcanoes can only erupt once.

Volcanoes can erupt multiple times. Some volcanoes erupt frequently, while others may remain dormant for hundreds or even thousands of years before erupting again. **False**

Fact: Lightning can strike the same place twice.

Lightning can strike the same place multiple times, especially tall, pointed, and isolated objects such as skyscrapers, trees, and lightning rods. **True**

Fact: Wildfires are only caused by human activity.

Wildfires can be caused by both natural events, such as lightning strikes, and human activities, such as unattended campfires, discarded cigarettes, and arson. **False**

Fact: *Floods are the most common natural disaster.*

Floods are indeed the most common natural disaster and can occur anywhere in the world. They can result from heavy rainfall, storm surges, melting snow, or dam failures. **True**

Fact: *Droughts happen overnight.*

Droughts develop over a long period, usually months or years, as a result of prolonged dry conditions and insufficient rainfall. **False**

Fact: *Avalanches can be triggered by loud noises.*

Loud noises, such as shouting or explosions, are unlikely to trigger avalanches. Most avalanches are caused by factors like heavy snowfall, rapid temperature changes, and disturbances in the snowpack. **False**

5.2 The Water Cycle

Water Cycle Facts: Learn fascinating facts about how water moves through the environment and its importance to life on Earth.

Fact: *Water in the water cycle only moves through oceans and rivers.*

Water in the water cycle moves through various stages and locations, including oceans, rivers, lakes, the atmosphere, and underground reservoirs. **False**

Fact: *Evaporation occurs only in warm weather.*

Evaporation, the process where water turns into vapor and rises into the atmosphere, can occur in any weather, not just warm. It happens whenever water is present, though it occurs more quickly in warmer conditions. **False**

Fact: *Clouds form because of condensation.*

Clouds form when water vapor in the air cools and condenses into tiny droplets or ice crystals. This process is known as condensation. **True**

Fact: *Precipitation can only occur as rain.*

Precipitation can occur in various forms, including rain, snow, sleet, and hail, depending on the temperature and atmospheric conditions. **False**

Fact: Plants contribute to the water cycle through a process called transpiration.

Plants take in water through their roots and release water vapor into the air from their leaves in a process called transpiration, which is a significant part of the water cycle. **True**

Fact: The water you drink today may have been part of a dinosaur's drinking supply millions of years ago.

The water on Earth is constantly recycled through the water cycle, meaning the water we use today has been around for millions of years and could have been consumed by dinosaurs. **True**

Fact: *Groundwater is not part of the water cycle.*

Groundwater, water stored underground in soil and rock layers, is an essential part of the water cycle. It can be accessed by plants and can replenish rivers, lakes, and wells. **False**

Fact: *All water eventually ends up in the ocean.*

While a significant amount of water does eventually flow into the oceans, water can also become trapped in glaciers, lakes, underground aquifers, and the atmosphere. **False**

Fact: *The Sun is the primary energy source driving the water cycle.*

The Sun provides the energy needed for evaporation, which drives the water cycle. Without the Sun's heat, the water cycle would not function. **True**

5.3 Weather and Climate

Weather Facts: Discover amazing facts about different weather phenomena, such as hurricanes, tornadoes, and blizzards.

Fact: *Weather and climate are the same thing.*

Weather refers to the short-term conditions of the atmosphere at a specific place and time, such as temperature, humidity, and precipitation. Climate, on the other hand, describes the average weather conditions in a region over a long period, typically 30 years or more. **False**

Fact: *The highest recorded temperature on Earth was in Death Valley, California.*

Death Valley holds the record for the highest temperature ever recorded on Earth, reaching 134 degrees Fahrenheit (56.7 degrees Celsius) on July 10, 1913. **True**

Fact: *The Earth's tilt is responsible for the changing seasons.*

The tilt of the Earth's axis causes the different seasons. As the Earth orbits the Sun, the tilt causes different parts of the Earth to receive varying amounts of sunlight throughout the year, leading to seasonal changes. **True**

Fact: *Climate change only affects temperatures.*

Climate change affects more than just temperatures. It can lead to changes in precipitation patterns, more extreme weather events, rising sea levels, and disruptions to ecosystems and agriculture. **False**

Fact: *A blizzard requires heavy snowfall to be classified as such.*

A blizzard is characterized by strong winds, low visibility, and blowing snow. While heavy snowfall can occur during a blizzard, it is not a requirement. The main factors are wind speed and visibility. **False**

Fact: *The polar regions are warming faster than the rest of the Earth.*

The polar regions, especially the Arctic, are experiencing warming at a rate faster than the global average. This phenomenon is known as polar amplification and is linked to feedback mechanisms like the loss of sea ice. ***True***

Fact: *Hurricanes only form over warm ocean waters.*

Hurricanes, also known as typhoons or cyclones in different regions, form over warm ocean waters. The warm water provides the energy needed for the storm to develop and intensify. **True**

Fact: *The eye of a hurricane is the most dangerous part.*

The eye of a hurricane is actually the calmest part of the storm, with clear skies and light winds. The most dangerous part is the eyewall, which surrounds the eye and has the strongest winds and heaviest rain. **False**

5.4 Ecosystems and Habitats

What is an Ecosystem?: Learn about different ecosystems, including forests, deserts, oceans, and wetlands.

Fact: *Coral reefs are often referred to as the "rainforests of the sea."*

Coral reefs are called the "rainforests of the sea" because of their incredible biodiversity. They are home to about 25% of all marine species, despite covering less than 1% of the ocean floor. **True**

Fact: *Deserts are always hot.*

Deserts are not always hot. While many are scorching during the day, some deserts, like the Gobi Desert, can be very cold, especially at night and during winter. **False**

Fact: *Wetlands are among the most productive ecosystems in the world.*

Wetlands are incredibly productive ecosystems, providing habitat for a wide range of species and offering essential services like water filtration, flood protection, and carbon storage. **True**

Fact: *Grasslands can only be found in Africa.*

Grasslands, known as savannas in Africa, can be found on every continent except Antarctica. They are called prairies in North America, steppes in Eurasia, and pampas in South America. **False**

Fact: *Tundra ecosystems have a high diversity of plant and animal species.*

Tundra ecosystems are characterized by their cold climate and low biodiversity. Few plant and animal species can survive the harsh conditions and short growing seasons. **False**

Fact: *Mangrove forests can only grow in saltwater environments.*

Mangrove forests thrive in coastal areas where saltwater meets freshwater. Their unique root systems allow them to tolerate and thrive in salty conditions. **True**

Fact: *Temperate forests experience all four seasons.*

Temperate forests, found in regions like North America, Europe, and Asia, experience all four seasons: winter, spring, summer, and fall, each bringing different conditions and changes in the ecosystem. **True**

Fact: *The Amazon Rainforest produces 20% of the world's oxygen.*

The Amazon Rainforest is often called the "lungs of the Earth" and plays a crucial role in producing oxygen and absorbing carbon dioxide. However, it produces about 6-9% of the world's oxygen, not 20%. **False**

Fact: *The largest ecosystem on Earth is the ocean.*

The ocean is the largest ecosystem on Earth, covering about 71% of the planet's surface. It supports a vast array of life forms and plays a critical role in regulating the Earth's climate. **True**

CHAPTER 6: HISTORY'S MYSTERIES

6.1 The Pyramids of Egypt

Fact: *The Pyramids of Giza were once surrounded by water.*

There is evidence that the area around the Pyramids of Giza was once much wetter than it is today. Ancient canals and harbors have been discovered, suggesting that the pyramids may have been accessible by boat. **True**

Fact: *The Pyramids of Egypt are aligned with the stars in Orion's Belt.*

The three pyramids of Giza are thought to be aligned with the three stars in Orion's Belt. This alignment might reflect the ancient Egyptians' belief in the significance of these stars and their connection to Osiris, the god of the afterlife. **True**

Fact: *The Riddle of the Sphinx is about the stages of human life.*

The Riddle of the Sphinx from Greek mythology asks, "What walks on four legs in the morning, two legs at noon, and three legs in the evening?" The answer is a human: a baby crawls on all fours, an adult walks on two legs, and an elderly person uses a cane. **True**

6.2 Stonehenge

Fact: *The exact purpose of Stonehenge remains unknown.*

The exact purpose of Stonehenge is still a mystery. It is believed to have been used for various purposes, including as a burial ground, a ceremonial site, and an astronomical observatory to mark solstices and equinoxes. **True**

Fact: *Stonehenge was built in a single phase of construction.*

Stonehenge was constructed in several phases over many centuries. The initial construction began around 3100 BCE, and modifications and additions continued until about 1600 BCE. **False**

Fact: *The stones of Stonehenge were transported over 200 miles.*

Some of the stones used in the construction of Stonehenge, specifically the smaller bluestones, were transported from the Preseli Hills in Wales, which is about 200 miles away from the site. **True**

Fact: *The alignment of Stonehenge is perfect for observing solar and lunar events.*

Stonehenge is aligned with the movements of the sun and the moon, which suggests that it was used for astronomical observations. **True**

6.3 The Lost City of Atlantis

Fact: *The story of Atlantis was first told by the philosopher Plato.*
The story of Atlantis comes from the ancient Greek philosopher Plato, who described it in his dialogues "Timaeus" and "Critias." According to Plato, Atlantis was a powerful and advanced civilization that sank into the ocean in a single day and night. **True**

Fact: *Most historians believe Atlantis was located in the Pacific Ocean.*
While the exact location of Atlantis remains a mystery, most historians and scholars who consider the tale to be based on some reality suggest it was located in the Atlantic Ocean. Various theories place it near the Mediterranean, the Canary Islands, or even under Antarctica's ice, but not the Pacific Ocean. **False**

Fact: *There is archaeological evidence that proves Atlantis existed.*
There is no definitive archaeological evidence that proves the existence of Atlantis. While many theories and sites have been proposed, including the island of Santorini and the Bimini Road, none have been conclusively linked to Atlantis. **False**

6.4 The Mystery of King Tutankhamun

Fact: King Tutankhamun became pharaoh at a very young age.

King Tutankhamun, often referred to as King Tut, became pharaoh at the young age of 9 or 10. He ruled Egypt during the 18th dynasty and reigned for about 10 years until his death at around 19 years old. **True**

Fact: King Tutankhamun's tomb was discovered in the Valley of the Queens.

King Tutankhamun's tomb, famously known as KV62, was discovered in the Valley of the Kings by British archaeologist Howard Carter in 1922. The tomb was remarkably well-preserved and contained numerous artifacts, including Tutankhamun's iconic gold mask. **False**

Fact: The cause of King Tutankhamun's death remains a mystery.

The exact cause of King Tutankhamun's death is still debated among historians and scientists. Various theories suggest he might have died from an infection caused by a broken leg, malaria, genetic disorders, or even murder. Modern technology has helped to provide clues, but the true cause remains uncertain. **True**

6.5 The Disappearance of the Dinosaurs

Fact: *Dinosaurs disappeared due to a single asteroid impact.*

The most widely accepted theory is that a massive asteroid impact caused the extinction of the dinosaurs about 66 million years ago. This impact created the Chicxulub crater in present-day Mexico and led to drastic environmental changes, but it is also believed that volcanic activity and climate changes may have contributed to their extinction. **Unknown**

Fact: *All species of dinosaurs went extinct at the same time.*

Not all species of dinosaurs went extinct simultaneously. While the mass extinction event significantly impacted most dinosaur species, some groups, like birds, which are considered modern-day dinosaurs, survived and continue to thrive. **False**

Fact: *The extinction of the dinosaurs allowed mammals to become the dominant land animals.*

After the extinction of the dinosaurs, mammals began to evolve and diversify rapidly, eventually becoming the dominant land animals. This transition allowed for the development of many new species, including primates, from which humans eventually evolved. **True**

6.6 The Secrets of the Bermuda Triangle

Fact: *The Bermuda Triangle is located between Florida, Bermuda, and Puerto Rico.*
The Bermuda Triangle is indeed located in the western part of the North Atlantic Ocean, roughly forming a triangle with its points at Miami, Bermuda, and Puerto Rico. This region is infamous for the mysterious disappearances of ships and aircraft. **True**

Fact: *All disappearances in the Bermuda Triangle have been proven to be caused by supernatural forces.*
Despite many theories and speculations, there is no scientific evidence that supernatural forces are responsible for the disappearances in the Bermuda Triangle. Most disappearances can be attributed to natural causes such as severe weather, human error, and mechanical failures. **False**

Fact: *The first recorded incident in the Bermuda Triangle occurred in the 1940s.*
The Bermuda Triangle gained widespread attention after the disappearance of Flight 19, a group of U.S. Navy bombers, in 1945. However, mysterious incidents in the area were recorded long before that, with reports dating back to the time of Christopher Columbus. **False**

6.7 The Voyages of the Vikings

Fact: *The Vikings only traveled as far as their neighboring countries in Scandinavia.*
The Vikings were known for their extensive travels and explorations. They ventured far beyond Scandinavia, reaching as far as North America, the British Isles, Greenland, Iceland, and even parts of Russia and the Mediterranean. **False**

Fact: *The Vikings used sophisticated navigational tools for their long voyages.*
The Vikings were skilled navigators who used various methods to find their way across the seas. They used the sun, stars, and landmarks, and some historians believe they might have used sunstones (a type of crystal) to locate the sun on cloudy days. **True**

Fact: *Leif Erikson is believed to have discovered America before Christopher Columbus.*
Leif Erikson, a Norse explorer, is believed to have landed in North America around the year 1000, nearly 500 years before Christopher Columbus. The site of his landing is thought to be in present-day Newfoundland, Canada, at a place called Vinland. **True**

6.8 The Enigma of Easter Island

Fact: The Moai statues on Easter Island were carved to honor ancestors.

The Moai statues, which are scattered across Easter Island, were indeed carved by the Rapa Nui people to honor their ancestors. These statues, some of which are up to 33 feet tall and weigh over 80 tons, are believed to represent the deified ancestors of the island's inhabitants. **True**

Fact: The Moai statues all face outwards towards the sea.

Most of the Moai statues actually face inland rather than towards the sea. They are positioned this way to watch over the villages, serving as protectors and symbols of authority for the island's communities. **False**

Fact: The construction and transportation of the Moai statues remain a complete mystery.

While there are many theories, the exact methods used by the Rapa Nui people to carve, transport, and erect the Moai statues are still debated. Some suggest they used a combination of log rollers, ropes, and human labor to move the statues from the quarries to their platforms, but the full details of their methods remain unknown. **True**

6.9 The Legend of the Loch Ness Monster

Fact: *The first recorded sighting of the Loch Ness Monster was in the 6th century.*
The first recorded sighting of the Loch Ness Monster dates back to the 6th century. An Irish monk named Saint Columba is said to have encountered a large beast in the River Ness, which flows into Loch Ness in Scotland. **True**

Fact: *The Loch Ness Monster is proven to be a prehistoric dinosaur.*
There is no scientific evidence proving that the Loch Ness Monster is a prehistoric dinosaur or any other creature. Despite numerous sightings and claims, most evidence, including photos and sonar readings, remains inconclusive or has been debunked. **False**

Fact: *Modern sonar technology has provided clear evidence of the Loch Ness Monster's existence.*
Modern sonar technology has been used to search the depths of Loch Ness, but it has not provided definitive proof of the monster's existence. While there have been some intriguing sonar contacts, none have conclusively identified a large, unknown creature. **False**

6.10 The Building of the Great Wall of China

Fact: *The Great Wall of China was built during a single dynasty.*
The Great Wall of China was constructed over several dynasties. The earliest walls were built as early as the 7th century BCE, but the most well-known sections were constructed during the Ming Dynasty (1368–1644 CE). **False**

Fact: *The Great Wall of China can be seen from space with the naked eye.*
The claim that the Great Wall of China can be seen from space with the naked eye is a myth. While it is an incredibly long structure, it is not visible to the unaided eye from space. Astronauts in low Earth orbit can sometimes see it with the help of binoculars or other equipment. **False**

Fact: *The primary purpose of the Great Wall was to protect against invasions.*
The Great Wall of China was primarily built to protect against invasions and raids by nomadic tribes from the north, such as the Mongols. It also served as a means of border control, allowing for the imposition of duties on goods transported along the Silk Road. **True**

6.11 The Mystery of Machu Picchu

Fact: *Machu Picchu was discovered by an explorer named Hiram Bingham.*
Machu Picchu was brought to international attention by American explorer Hiram Bingham in 1911. He was led to the site by local indigenous farmers and then documented his findings, which sparked global interest in this ancient Incan city. **True**

Fact: *Machu Picchu was built as a military fortress.*
Machu Picchu is believed to have been built as an estate for the Inca emperor Pachacuti. While it may have had some defensive features, its primary purpose was likely ceremonial and residential, serving as a retreat and a site for religious activities. **False**

Fact: *The precise stonework at Machu Picchu was done without the use of mortar.*
The Inca used a technique called "ashlar masonry," where stones are cut to fit together perfectly without the use of mortar. This method provided stability in an earthquake-prone region, and the stones have remained tightly in place for centuries. **True**

6.12 The Secrets of the Nazca Lines

Fact: The Nazca Lines were created by removing a layer of reddish-brown pebbles to reveal the lighter soil underneath.

The Nazca Lines, located in the Nazca Desert of southern Peru, were created by removing the top layer of reddish-brown iron oxide-coated pebbles to reveal the lighter-colored earth beneath. This method created the contrasting lines that form various shapes and figures. **True**

Fact: The Nazca Lines can only be seen from the ground.

The Nazca Lines are best viewed from the air due to their massive scale. Some of the figures span hundreds of meters, making it difficult to fully appreciate their designs from the ground. Small hills and elevated areas nearby also offer partial views. **False**

Fact: The purpose of the Nazca Lines remains a mystery, but some theories suggest they were used for astronomical and religious purposes.

The exact purpose of the Nazca Lines is still debated among researchers. Some theories suggest they were used for astronomical purposes, aligning with celestial events, while others propose they were part of religious or ceremonial practices to honor deities and request water in the arid desert. **True**

6.13 The Legend of El Dorado

Fact: *El Dorado refers to a city made entirely of gold.*

The legend of El Dorado originally referred to a person, not a city. El Dorado, meaning "The Golden One," was believed to be a Muisca tribal chief who covered himself in gold dust and submerged in Lake Guatavita as part of a ritual. Over time, the story evolved to describe a mythical city of immense wealth. **False**

Fact: *The search for El Dorado led to numerous expeditions in South America.*

The legend of El Dorado inspired many explorers, including Sir Walter Raleigh and Gonzalo Pizarro, to embark on perilous expeditions in search of this fabled city of gold. These quests often led them deep into the uncharted jungles and mountains of South America, but no city of gold was ever found. **True**

Fact: *Modern historians believe El Dorado was located in the Amazon rainforest.*

Most historians now believe that El Dorado was a myth rather than a real place. The story likely originated from the rituals of the Muisca people and was exaggerated by early Spanish explorers. While the exact location of El Dorado remains a mystery, it is generally considered a legend rather than a historical fact. **True**

6.14 The Mystery of the Mary Celeste

Fact: *The Mary Celeste was found completely abandoned with no sign of the crew.*

The Mary Celeste, a merchant ship, was discovered adrift in the Atlantic Ocean on December 4, 1872, with no one on board. The ship was in good condition, and all personal belongings and cargo were intact, but the crew had vanished without a trace. **True**

Fact: *The ship showed clear signs of a pirate attack.*

There was no evidence of a pirate attack on the Mary Celeste. The ship's cargo, including valuable alcohol, was untouched, and there were no signs of struggle or violence, making a pirate attack unlikely. **False**

Fact: *The mystery of the Mary Celeste has been conclusively solved.*

The mystery of the Mary Celeste remains unsolved to this day. Various theories have been proposed, including mutiny, piracy, natural disasters, and even sea monsters, but none have been proven. The fate of the crew continues to be one of maritime history's greatest enigmas. **False**

6.15 The Legend of Robin Hood

Fact: *Robin Hood is said to have lived in Sherwood Forest.*

According to the legend, Robin Hood lived in Sherwood Forest, near the city of Nottingham in England. He is famously known for his adventures in this forest, where he and his band of Merry Men would rob the rich and give to the poor. **True**

Fact: *The earliest tales of Robin Hood were written during the reign of King Richard the Lionheart.*

The earliest tales of Robin Hood were written several centuries after King Richard the Lionheart, during the late Middle Ages. While King Richard appears in some versions of the story, the legend of Robin Hood evolved over time through ballads, poems, and later, plays and novels. **False**

Fact: *Maid Marian is a later addition to the Robin Hood legend.*

Maid Marian, Robin Hood's love interest, was not part of the earliest tales of Robin Hood. She was added to the legend later, becoming a central character in the stories during the 16th century, contributing to the romantic aspect of the legend. **True**

6.16 The Mystery of the Holy Grail

Fact: *The Holy Grail is believed to be the cup used by Jesus at the Last Supper.*
The Holy Grail is traditionally believed to be the cup that Jesus Christ used at the Last Supper. According to legend, it was later used by Joseph of Arimathea to collect Jesus' blood at the crucifixion. **True**

Fact: *The Holy Grail has been definitively found and identified.*
Despite numerous claims and theories, the Holy Grail has never been definitively found or identified. Various artifacts have been suggested as the Holy Grail, but none have been universally accepted as the true cup. **False**

Fact: *The search for the Holy Grail has inspired many literary and historical quests.*
The legend of the Holy Grail has inspired countless stories, books, and movies, including the famous tales of King Arthur and the Knights of the Round Table. These stories often depict the quest for the Holy Grail as a noble and challenging adventure. **True**

6.17 The Legend of the Fountain of Youth

Fact: *The Fountain of Youth is said to restore the youth of anyone who drinks from it.*
According to legend, the Fountain of Youth is a magical spring that restores the youth of anyone who drinks or bathes in its waters. This mythical fountain has been sought by explorers for centuries, hoping to find eternal youth. **True**

Fact: *The Spanish explorer Ponce de León discovered the Fountain of Youth in Florida.*
The Spanish explorer Juan Ponce de León is often linked to the search for the Fountain of Youth, and many stories suggest he discovered it in Florida. However, historical evidence shows that while he explored Florida in 1513, there is no solid proof that he was specifically searching for the Fountain of Youth. **False**

Fact: *The idea of a Fountain of Youth exists in various cultures around the world.*
The concept of a Fountain of Youth is not unique to Western legend. Many cultures have myths and stories about magical waters that grant eternal youth and health, including tales from ancient China and Japan, indicating a widespread fascination with the idea of rejuvenation. **True**

CHAPTER 7: INCREDIBLE INVENTIONS

7.1 The Wheel: Rolling Into History

Fact: *The wheel was invented in ancient Egypt for building the pyramids.*
The wheel was not invented in ancient Egypt for building the pyramids. The ancient Egyptians used sleds and manpower to move large stones. The wheel was actually invented around 3500 BCE in Mesopotamia for pottery and later adapted for use in transportation.
False

Fact: *The first wheels were used for making pottery, not for transportation.*
The first wheels were indeed used for making pottery. The potter's wheel, which appeared around 3500 BCE in Mesopotamia, was one of the earliest applications of the wheel, helping artisans shape clay more efficiently. **True**

Fact: *The invention of the wheel led to significant advancements in agriculture.*
The invention of the wheel greatly advanced agriculture by making it possible to create plows and carts. These tools helped farmers cultivate larger fields and transport goods more easily, leading to increased productivity and the growth of civilizations. **True**

7.2 The Printing Press: Spreading Knowledge

Fact: *The printing press was invented by Johannes Gutenberg in the 15th century.*
The printing press was indeed invented by Johannes Gutenberg in the mid-15th century. His invention of movable type printing revolutionized the production of books, making them more accessible and affordable, which in turn helped spread knowledge and literacy across Europe. **True**

Fact: *Before the printing press, books were commonly printed using woodblock printing.*
Before the invention of the printing press, books were often made using woodblock printing. This method involved carving an entire page of text or images onto a block of wood, inking it, and pressing it onto paper. **True**

Fact: *The first book printed using Gutenberg's printing press was "The Adventures of Robin Hood."*
The first major book printed using Gutenberg's printing press was the Gutenberg Bible, not "The Adventures of Robin Hood." The Gutenberg Bible, also known as the 42-line Bible, was completed around 1455 and is considered one of the greatest achievements in printing history. **False**

7.3 The Telephone: Connecting the World

Fact: *Alexander Graham Bell invented the telephone in the 19th century.*

Alexander Graham Bell is credited with inventing the first practical telephone. He was awarded the first US patent for the invention of the telephone in 1876. Bell's invention revolutionized communication, allowing people to speak to each other over long distances for the first time. **True**

Fact: *The first words spoken on the telephone were "Hello, can you hear me?"*

The first words spoken on the telephone by Alexander Graham Bell were actually "Mr. Watson, come here, I want to see you." He said this to his assistant, Thomas Watson, on March 10, 1876. This moment marked the first successful use of the telephone. **False**

Fact: *The rotary dial telephone was introduced before the push-button telephone.*

The rotary dial telephone was introduced in the early 20th century, well before the push-button telephone. The rotary dial allowed users to make calls by turning a dial for each digit of the phone number. Push-button telephones, which used touch-tone dialing, were introduced later, in the 1960s. **True**

7.4 The Airplane: Taking to the Skies

Fact: *The Wright brothers made the first successful powered flight in 1903.*
The Wright brothers, Orville and Wilbur, made the first successful powered flight on December 17, 1903, in Kitty Hawk, North Carolina. Their airplane, the Wright Flyer, stayed aloft for 12 seconds and covered 120 feet. This historic flight marked the beginning of aviation.
True

Fact: *The first airplanes were used primarily for commercial passenger flights.*
The first airplanes were not used primarily for commercial passenger flights. Initially, airplanes were used for military purposes, mail delivery, and exploration. Commercial passenger flights became more common in the 1920s and 1930s as aviation technology advanced.
False

Fact: *Amelia Earhart was the first person to fly solo nonstop across the Atlantic Ocean.*
Amelia Earhart was not the first person but the first woman to fly solo nonstop across the Atlantic Ocean. She achieved this historic flight on May 20-21, 1932, five years after Charles Lindbergh became the first person to do so in 1927. Earhart's flight cemented her legacy as a pioneering aviator. **False**

7.5 The Internet: Connecting Everyone

Fact: *The Internet was invented in the 1990s.*
The foundations of the Internet were actually developed much earlier, in the 1960s. The 1990s saw the commercialization and rapid expansion of the Internet, but its origins trace back to the ARPANET, a project initiated by the U.S. Department of Defense. **False**

Fact: *The World Wide Web and the Internet are the same thing.*
The World Wide Web (WWW) and the Internet are not the same thing. The Internet is the global network of interconnected computers, while the World Wide Web is a system of interlinked hypertext documents accessed via the Internet. The Web was invented by Tim Berners-Lee in 1989. **False**

Fact: *The first website ever created is still online.*
The first website, created by Tim Berners-Lee in 1991, is still online. It was a simple page explaining the World Wide Web project, how to use a browser, and how to set up a web server. **True**

Fact: *Email was one of the first services available on the Internet.*
The first significant use of email dates back to the early 1970s, and it quickly became a fundamental tool for communication across the burgeoning Internet. **True**

7.6 The Computer: Revolutionizing Technology

Fact: The first computers were developed in the 20th century.

The first electronic computers were indeed developed in the 20th century. One of the earliest was the ENIAC (Electronic Numerical Integrator and Computer), which was completed in 1945. These early computers were massive machines, filling entire rooms and using vacuum tubes for processing. **True**

Fact: The first personal computer was created by Apple.

The first personal computer, the Altair 8800, was released by MITS (Micro Instrumentation and Telemetry Systems) in 1975. While Apple's Apple II, released in 1977, was one of the first highly successful personal computers, it was not the first one created. **False**

Fact: Computers can only perform tasks if they are programmed to do so.

Computers operate based on instructions given by software programs. They can only perform tasks that are explicitly programmed by humans. This means that without specific instructions, a computer cannot perform any function. **True**

7.7 The Automobile: Changing the Way We Travel

Fact: *The first gasoline-powered automobile was invented by Karl Benz.*

Karl Benz invented the first practical gasoline-powered automobile in 1885. His invention, the Benz Patent-Motorwagen, had a single-cylinder engine and is widely regarded as the first car designed to generate its own power. **True**

Fact: *Henry Ford invented the first automobile.*

Henry Ford did not invent the first automobile, but he revolutionized the automobile industry by introducing assembly line production. This method significantly reduced the cost of manufacturing, making cars affordable for many people. His Model T, introduced in 1908, became the first widely accessible automobile. **False**

Fact: *The first electric cars were developed in the 1990s.*

Electric cars date back much earlier than the 1990s. The first electric vehicles were developed in the early 19th century. In fact, electric cars were quite popular in the late 1800s and early 1900s before gasoline-powered cars became dominant. **False**

7.8 The Television: Bringing Stories to Life

Fact: The first electronic television was invented by Philo Farnsworth.

Philo Farnsworth is credited with inventing the first fully functional all-electronic television system. He demonstrated the first working model of his television in 1927, revolutionizing the way we consume visual entertainment. **True**

Fact: Color television was available as soon as the first televisions were invented.

Color television did not become widely available until the 1950s, several decades after the invention of the first black-and-white televisions. The first successful color television broadcast was made by NBC in 1954. **False**

Fact: The largest television screen in the world is over 3,000 square feet.

The largest television screen in the world, located in Times Square, New York City, measures over 11,000 square feet. This massive screen, known as the "Mega LED Display," is used for advertising and broadcasting events. **True**

7.9 The Microwave Oven: Heating Up the Kitchen

Fact: *The microwave oven was invented accidentally by a scientist working on radar technology.*

The microwave oven was indeed invented accidentally by Percy Spencer, an engineer working on radar technology during World War II. He noticed that a chocolate bar in his pocket melted while he was working with a magnetron, leading to the discovery of microwave cooking. **True**

Fact: *The first microwave ovens were very affordable and quickly became popular in households.*

The first microwave ovens, introduced in the late 1940s and early 1950s, were actually very expensive and quite large, making them impractical for most households. It wasn't until the 1970s that microwave ovens became more affordable and compact, leading to widespread adoption in homes. **False**

Fact: *Microwaves heat food from the inside out.*

Microwaves heat food by causing water molecules in the food to vibrate, producing heat. This process starts at the surface and moves inward, which is why some foods can heat unevenly, with the outer layers becoming hot while the inside remains cool. **False**

7.10 The Space Shuttle: Exploring Beyond Earth

Fact: *The space shuttle was the first reusable spacecraft.*

The space shuttle was indeed the first reusable spacecraft. Developed by NASA, it could be launched into space, return to Earth, and be prepared for another mission. This design revolutionized space travel by reducing the cost of sending humans and cargo into space.
True

Fact: *The first space shuttle to orbit the Earth was named "Enterprise."*

The first space shuttle built was named "Enterprise," but it never orbited the Earth. It was used for test flights within the atmosphere. The first space shuttle to orbit the Earth was "Columbia," which launched on April 12, 1981, marking the beginning of the Space Shuttle program.
False

Fact: *The space shuttle program was responsible for building the International Space Station (ISS).*

The space shuttle program played a crucial role in the construction and servicing of the International Space Station. Shuttle missions delivered key components, supplies, and astronauts to the ISS, contributing significantly to its assembly and ongoing operations. **True**

7.11 The Submarine: Exploring the Depths

Fact: *The first military submarine was built during the American Revolutionary War.*
The first military submarine, named the Turtle, was built during the American Revolutionary War by David Bushnell in 1775. It was designed to attach explosives to enemy ships and was used in an attempt to break the British naval blockade. **True**

Fact: *Submarines can only operate in shallow waters due to pressure limits.*
Modern submarines are capable of operating at significant depths thanks to advanced engineering. Military submarines, like those used by navies, can dive to depths of over 800 feet (240 meters) or more, and some research submarines can reach the deep ocean floors. **False**

Fact: *Nuclear-powered submarines can remain submerged for months without resurfacing.*
Nuclear-powered submarines have a significant advantage over diesel-electric submarines because they do not need to surface frequently for air. They can remain submerged for months at a time, limited mainly by the need for food and supplies for the crew. **True**

7.12 The Refrigerator: Keeping Things Cool

Fact: *The first household refrigerators were powered by electricity.*

The first household refrigerators, introduced in the early 20th century, were indeed powered by electricity. These early models revolutionized food storage by allowing people to keep perishable items fresh for longer periods, making daily life more convenient. **True**

Fact: *Before refrigerators, people used natural ice and iceboxes to keep food cold.*

Before the invention of modern refrigerators, people used iceboxes to keep their food cold. These iceboxes were insulated cabinets that held large blocks of ice, which needed to be replaced regularly as they melted. This method helped preserve food but required a steady supply of natural ice. **True**

Fact: *Modern refrigerators use Freon as a coolant.*

Most modern refrigerators no longer use Freon as a coolant due to its harmful effects on the ozone layer. Instead, they use more environmentally friendly refrigerants, such as HFCs (hydrofluorocarbons), which have a lower impact on the environment. **False**

7.13 The Bicycle: Pedaling Forward

Fact: *The first bicycles were called "velocipedes" and had no pedals.*
The earliest bicycles, known as "velocipedes" or "draisines," were invented in the early 19th century and had no pedals. Riders would push themselves along with their feet on the ground. Pedals were added later, in the 1860s, leading to the development of the modern bicycle. **True**

Fact: *Bicycles are only used for transportation and recreation, not for competitive sports.*
Bicycles are widely used for competitive sports as well as for transportation and recreation. Cycling competitions, such as the Tour de France, are among the most popular and prestigious sporting events in the world. **False**

Fact: *The invention of the safety bicycle in the late 1800s made cycling more accessible and popular.*
The safety bicycle, invented in the late 1800s, featured equal-sized wheels and a chain-driven rear wheel, making it much more stable and easier to ride than earlier models with a large front wheel. This design greatly increased the popularity and accessibility of cycling. **True**

7.14 The Radio: Airwaves and Communication

Fact: *Guglielmo Marconi is credited with inventing the radio.*
Guglielmo Marconi is indeed credited with inventing the radio. In the late 19th century, he developed the first successful long-distance wireless telegraph and transmitted the first radio signal across the Atlantic Ocean in 1901, revolutionizing communication. **True**

Fact: *The first radio broadcasts were used primarily for entertainment and music.*
The earliest radio broadcasts were actually used for transmitting news and information rather than entertainment. It wasn't until the 1920s that radio stations began regularly broadcasting music, drama, and other entertainment programs, which quickly gained popularity. **False**

Fact: *Radios only became widely used in homes after World War II.*
Radios became widely used in homes well before World War II. By the 1920s and 1930s, radio ownership had become common, with families gathering around their radios to listen to news, entertainment, and music programs. The radio played a crucial role in providing information and entertainment during the war. **False**

7.15 The Camera: Capturing Moments

Fact: *The first photograph ever taken required an exposure time of several hours.*

The first photograph ever taken, by Joseph Nicéphore Niépce in 1826, required an exposure time of about eight hours. This early process, known as heliography, used a pewter plate coated with bitumen and required long exposure to capture an image. **True**

Fact: *Digital cameras were invented in the 1980s.*

The first digital camera was actually invented in 1975 by Steven Sasson, an engineer at Eastman Kodak. It was a prototype that took 23 seconds to capture a single image and recorded it on a cassette tape. Digital cameras became more widely available to consumers in the 1990s. **False**

Fact: *The term "camera" comes from the Latin phrase "camera obscura," meaning "dark room."*

The term "camera" does indeed come from the Latin phrase "camera obscura," which means "dark room." Camera obscura was an early optical device that projected an image of its surroundings onto a screen and was used as a drawing aid by artists. This concept eventually led to the development of the modern camera. **True**

7.16 The Sewing Machine: Stitching Together History

Fact: *The first sewing machine was invented by Elias Howe in 1846.*
Elias Howe is credited with inventing the first practical sewing machine in 1846. His machine could sew a straight seam using a lockstitch, which was a significant advancement in sewing technology and revolutionized the garment industry. **True**

Fact: *The first sewing machines were powered by electricity.*
The earliest sewing machines were not powered by electricity but were operated manually using a hand crank or a foot pedal, known as a treadle. Electric sewing machines became popular in the early 20th century, making sewing easier and faster. **False**

Fact: *Isaac Singer made significant improvements to the sewing machine and helped popularize it.*
Isaac Singer did indeed make significant improvements to the sewing machine, including the addition of the foot pedal for hands-free operation. He also implemented a business model that included installment payment plans, making sewing machines more accessible to the general public. **True**

7.17 The Washing Machine: Cleaning Made Easy

Fact: *The first washing machines were operated by hand and used a crank to agitate the clothes.*
The earliest washing machines were indeed operated by hand and used a crank mechanism to agitate the clothes. These manual machines, invented in the late 18th and early 19th centuries, made washing clothes easier than scrubbing them by hand on a washboard. **True**

Fact: *The first electric washing machine was invented in the early 1900s.*
The first electric washing machine, called the Thor, was introduced in 1908 by the Hurley Machine Company of Chicago. It featured a drum that could be powered by an electric motor, which significantly reduced the labor involved in washing clothes. **True**

Fact: *All washing machines use hot water to clean clothes effectively.*
Not all washing machines use hot water to clean clothes. Modern washing machines often have settings for cold, warm, and hot water, and many detergents are formulated to work effectively in cold water, saving energy and preventing colors from fading. **False**

CHAPTER 8: WORLD RECORDS AND UNBELIEVABLE ACHIEVEMENTS

8.1 Tallest and Smallest: Amazing Extremes

Fact: *The tallest tree in the world is named Hyperion.*

Hyperion, a coast redwood (Sequoia sempervirens) in California, is the tallest tree in the world. It stands at about 116 meters (380 feet) tall. Discovered in 2006, its exact location is kept secret to protect it from damage. **True**

Fact: *The smallest country in the world is Monaco.*

The smallest country in the world is actually Vatican City, not Monaco. Vatican City is an independent city-state enclaved within Rome, Italy, and covers just about 44 hectares (110 acres). **False**

Fact: *The shortest adult human ever recorded was Chandra Bahadur Dangi.*

Chandra Bahadur Dangi from Nepal holds the record for the shortest adult human, measuring just 54.6 centimeters (21.5 inches) in height. He held the record until his passing in 2015. **True**

Fact: *The world's smallest dog breed is the Chihuahua.*

The Chihuahua is the smallest dog breed in the world. These tiny dogs typically weigh between 1.5 to 3 kilograms (3.3 to 6.6 pounds) and stand about 15 to 23 centimeters (6 to 9 inches) tall. Despite their small size, they are known for their big personalities. **True**

Fact: *The largest flower in the world is the Titan Arum.*

The largest flower in the world is the Rafflesia arnoldii, not the Titan Arum. Rafflesia arnoldii can grow up to 1 meter (3.3 feet) in diameter and weighs up to 11 kilograms (24 pounds). It is known for its strong odor, similar to that of rotting flesh. **False**

Fact: *The tallest building in the world is the Burj Khalifa in Dubai.*

The Burj Khalifa in Dubai, United Arab Emirates, is the tallest building in the world. It stands at an astonishing 828 meters (2,717 feet) tall and has 163 floors. It was completed in 2010 and remains a marvel of modern engineering. **True**

Fact: *The tallest animal in the world is the giraffe.*

The giraffe is indeed the tallest animal in the world, with males reaching heights of up to 5.5 meters (18 feet). Their long necks allow them to reach leaves high up in trees, which other animals cannot access. **True**

Fact: The tallest roller coaster in the world is Kingda Ka.

Kingda Ka, located at Six Flags Great Adventure in New Jersey, USA, is the tallest roller coaster in the world. It stands 139 meters (456 feet) tall and launches riders at speeds up to 206 kilometers per hour (128 miles per hour). **True**

Fact: The tallest waterfall in the world is Angel Falls in Venezuela.

Angel Falls, located in Venezuela, is the tallest waterfall in the world. It has an uninterrupted drop of 807 meters (2,648 feet) and a total height of 979 meters (3,212 feet). Named after Jimmy Angel, the American aviator who discovered it, the waterfall is a breathtaking natural wonder. **True**

Fact: *The world's smallest bird is the bee hummingbird.*

The bee hummingbird, native to Cuba, is the smallest bird in the world. It measures about 5.5 centimeters (2.2 inches) in length and weighs around 1.6 grams (0.056 ounces). **True**

8.2 Fastest and Slowest: Speed Demons and Slowpokes

Fact: *The cheetah is the fastest land animal in the world.*

The cheetah is indeed the fastest land animal, capable of reaching speeds up to 70 miles per hour (113 kilometers per hour) in short bursts covering distances up to 500 meters (1,640 feet). This incredible speed helps them catch their prey in the wild. **True**

Fact: *The Galápagos tortoise is the slowest reptile.*

The Galápagos tortoise is one of the slowest reptiles, moving at a pace of about 0.3 kilometers per hour (0.19 miles per hour). These tortoises are known for their slow, steady movements and long lifespans. **True**

Fact: *The fastest fish in the ocean is the sailfish.*

The sailfish is the fastest fish in the ocean, capable of swimming at speeds up to 68 miles per hour (110 kilometers per hour). Its speed helps it catch prey and escape from predators. **True**

Fact: *The garden snail is the fastest snail species.*

The garden snail is not the fastest snail; it is one of the slowest. Snails, in general, are slow creatures, and the garden snail moves at a pace of about 0.03 miles per hour (0.048 kilometers per hour). **False**

Fact: *The fastest car in the world is the Bugatti Veyron.*

While the Bugatti Veyron was once the fastest car, the current record holder is the SSC Tuatara, which reached speeds of 282.9 miles per hour (455.3 kilometers per hour) in October 2020. **False**

Fact: *The slowest fish is the dwarf seahorse.*

The dwarf seahorse is indeed the slowest fish, moving at a speed of about 5 feet per hour (1.5 meters per hour). It relies on camouflage and gentle currents to move and find food. **True**

Fact: *The fastest human sprinter is Usain Bolt.*

Usain Bolt is the fastest human sprinter, holding the world record for the 100 meters with a time of 9.58 seconds. This record was set at the 2009 World Championships in Berlin. **True**

Fact: *The slowest mammal is the three-toed sloth.*

The three-toed sloth is the slowest mammal, moving at an average speed of about 0.24 kilometers per hour (0.15 miles per hour). They spend most of their time hanging from trees and moving very little, conserving energy. **True**

Fact: *The fastest bird in level flight is the common swift.*

The common swift holds the record for the fastest bird in level flight, reaching speeds of up to 69 miles per hour (111 kilometers per hour). Their aerodynamic bodies and strong wings make them incredibly fast flyers. **True**

8.3 Record-Breaking Feats of Strength and Endurance

Fact: *The longest someone has held a plank position is over 8 hours.*

The world record for the longest plank position is indeed over 8 hours. George Hood set the record in 2020 by holding the plank position for 8 hours, 15 minutes, and 15 seconds, showcasing incredible core strength and endurance. **True**

Fact: *The highest number of push-ups performed in one hour is 1,000.*

The record for the most push-ups performed in one hour is far higher. In 2022, Jarrad Young set the record by completing 3,182 push-ups in one hour. **False**

Fact: *The longest marathon run without sleep lasted more than 11 days.*

The longest recorded marathon run without sleep was by Randy Gardner, who stayed awake for 11 days and 25 minutes in 1964. This incredible feat demonstrated human endurance, though such attempts can be dangerous to health. **True**

Fact: *The heaviest weight ever lifted by a human is over 6,000 pounds.*

The heaviest weight ever lifted by a human in a single lift is significantly lower. The world record for the heaviest deadlift is held by Hafthor Bjornsson, who lifted 1,104 pounds (501 kilograms) in 2020. **False**

Fact: The longest distance swum without stopping is over 139 miles.

Chloe McCardel set the world record for the longest distance swum without stopping in open water, covering 139.8 miles (225 kilometers) in 2014. This record showcases incredible endurance and determination. **True**

Fact: The highest number of pull-ups performed in 24 hours is over 7,000.

The world record for the most pull-ups performed in 24 hours is indeed over 7,000. John Orth set the record by completing 7,600 pull-ups in 2016. **True**

Fact: The longest time spent in a static wall sit position is 1 hour.

The world record for the longest static wall sit is much longer. Dr. Thienna Ho holds the record, having maintained the wall sit position for 11 hours and 51 minutes in 2008. **False**

Fact: *The longest free dive without oxygen lasted over 11 minutes.*

The record for the longest free dive without oxygen is held by Aleix Segura Vendrell, who stayed underwater for an astonishing 24 minutes and 3 seconds in 2016, using pure oxygen before the dive. **True**

Fact: *The heaviest weight lifted by a single finger is 200 pounds.*

The heaviest weight lifted by a single finger is 242 pounds (110 kilograms), achieved by Steve Keeler in 2013. This feat required exceptional finger strength and endurance. **True**

Fact: *The longest time running on a treadmill is 24 hours.*

The longest time spent running on a treadmill is much longer than 24 hours. The record is held by Zach Bitter, who ran for 100 miles (161 kilometers) in 12 hours. **False**

8.4 Extraordinary Natural Phenomena

Fact: *Bioluminescent bays glow due to microorganisms in the water.*

Bioluminescent bays glow because of tiny microorganisms called dinoflagellates. When these organisms are disturbed by movement in the water, they emit light, creating a stunning glowing effect. **True**

Fact: *Blood Falls in Antarctica gets its red color from algae.*

Blood Falls in Antarctica gets its eerie red color from iron-rich saltwater that oxidizes and turns red when it comes into contact with the air. This phenomenon occurs as the iron-laden water emerges from the glacier. **False**

Fact: *The Rainbow Mountains are found in Australia.*

The Rainbow Mountains, known for their colorful striped appearance, are located in the Zhangye Danxia Landform Geological Park in China, not Australia. The vibrant colors are caused by the layering of sedimentary mineral deposits over millions of years. **False**

Fact: *The Northern Lights, or Aurora Borealis, are caused by solar wind particles colliding with Earth's atmosphere.*

The Northern Lights are created when charged particles from the Sun, known as the solar wind, collide with gases in Earth's atmosphere. This interaction causes beautiful light displays in the polar regions. **True**

Fact: *Rainbow eucalyptus trees have multicolored bark.*

Rainbow eucalyptus trees, native to the Philippines, Indonesia, and Papua New Guinea, have multicolored bark that peels away to reveal streaks of green, blue, orange, and purple. This unique feature makes them one of the most colorful trees in the world. **True**

Fact: *The Eye of the Sahara is a man-made structure.*

The Eye of the Sahara, also known as the Richat Structure, is a natural geological formation in Mauritania. Its circular shape, visible from space, was formed by erosion and geological uplift, not by human activity. **False**

Fact: *The Salar de Uyuni in Bolivia is the world's largest salt flat.*

Salar de Uyuni is the world's largest salt flat, spanning over 10,000 square kilometers (3,900 square miles) in Bolivia. During the rainy season, it transforms into a giant mirror, reflecting the sky beautifully. **True**

Fact: *The Giant's Causeway in Northern Ireland was formed by volcanic activity.*

The Giant's Causeway, with its unique hexagonal basalt columns, was formed by volcanic activity around 60 million years ago. As the lava cooled rapidly, it cracked into the distinctive shapes we see today. **True**

Fact: *Morning Glory clouds are a rare phenomenon found in Australia's Gulf of Carpentaria.*

Morning Glory clouds are rare, tubular cloud formations that can stretch up to 1,000 kilometers (620 miles). They are most commonly seen in the Gulf of Carpentaria in Northern Australia during the spring. **True**

CONCLUSION: KEEP CURIOUS!

As we reach the end of "Fascinating Facts for Smart Kids Ages 6-12 Years," we hope you've enjoyed this exciting journey through the amazing world of knowledge. From the mysteries of the universe to the wonders of our bodies, from incredible inventions to unbelievable achievements, this book has taken you on an adventure filled with fascinating discoveries.

The Quest for Knowledge

The facts in this book come from a variety of sources, including the vast resources of the internet, books, and expert contributions. Each fact has been carefully selected to ignite your curiosity and encourage a love for learning. But remember, these facts are just the

beginning. There is always more to discover and explore.

Keep Exploring

The world is full of endless wonders just waiting to be uncovered. Whether you are intrigued by nature, history, science, or technology, there is always something new to learn. Use the internet and books to dive deeper into topics that interest you. Visit libraries, museums, and websites to expand your knowledge even further.

Share Your Discoveries

One of the joys of learning new things is sharing them with others. Tell your friends and family about the amazing facts you've learned. Discuss your

favorite topics and ask them what they know. Sharing knowledge helps you remember what you've learned and spreads the joy of discovery.

Stay Curious

Curiosity is the key to lifelong learning. Never stop asking questions and seeking answers. The more curious you are, the more you will discover about the incredible world around us. There is always another mystery to solve, another fact to learn, and another adventure to embark on.

Thank You

Thank you for joining us on this fascinating journey through the world of knowledge. We hope this book has sparked your imagination, answered some of your questions, and inspired you to keep learning. The facts presented here are just a glimpse of the vast amount of information available from various online and offline sources.

So, keep reading, keep exploring, and always stay curious!

Michelle Burton

INDEX

Made in United States
Troutdale, OR
01/17/2025

28024617R00111